The Baker's Philosopher

The story of a simple craft shrouded in myths

Duncan Campbell

Published in Australia by Duncan Campbell

First published in Australia 2025

This edition published 2025

Copyright © Duncan Campbell 2025

Cover design, typesetting: WorkingType (www.workingtype.com.au)

The right of Duncan Campbell to be identified as the Author of the Work has been asserted in accordance with the Copyright, Designs and Patents Act 1988.

All rights reserved. No part of this publication may be reproduced, stored in a retrieval system, or transmitted, in any form or by any means without the prior written permission of the publisher, nor be otherwise circulated in any form of binding or cover other than that in which it is published and without a similar condition being imposed on the subsequent purchaser.

ISBN: 978-1-7641905-3-4

Other titles by Duncan Campbell

I dedicate this book to the following,

Heather Maliatto (Pastry Chef)– aged 32

Windows of the World Restaurant

World Trade Centre, New York.

Lost her life 11th September 2001

Renea Lau (Pastry Chef) – aged 32

Ganache chocolates

South Yarra,

Melbourne,

Lost her life July 28th 2014

Two young female pastry chefs living their dream, of which was savagely snatched away from them. Both talented in their chosen profession, both aiming for the same accolades of contentment and excelling their skills towards success, prosperity and the simplicity of pleasing others through work. Our thoughts remain with you always.

and

Gursimran Kaur

Deceased October 19th 2024 –

aged 19, Halifax , Nova Scotia , Canada)

Acknowledgements

*Thank you for all the Bakers, Pastrycooks, Confectioners
I have had the pleasure to work with and call my friends
and associates during my career.*

*The Bakery industry requires immense courage, determination
and servitude to achieve its daily bread.*

Comradeship is a necessity, friendship demanded, teamwork compliant.

The silent few who are worth more than any currency could evaluate.

Thank you from my heart, soul and spirit.

Content

1.	Baking Philosophy	1
2.	Its Just a Numbers Game	4
3.	What is Baking: Baker to Baker	5
4.	The Baking Bug	7
5.	Bakers Hands	8
6.	The Bakers Consensus	10
7.	Bread	12
8.	Bread	14
9.	The Bakehouse	18
10.	Baking Truths	21
11.	The Laws and Lores of Bakery	24
12.	Rules of Engagement	31
13.	Cake	44
14.	SPELT (An Ancient Grain)	47
15.	Community	49
16.	Sandwiches	50
17.	1758	52
18.	The Power of Pastry	54
19.	The Wonder of Plunder	56
20.	The Bakers Shift	58
21.	The Old Baker	60
22.	Hybrid doughs	63
23.	Bakers Prep List	65
24.	Dough Recipe	67
25.	X, ant	69
26.	Celebrity Bakers	72
27.	The Bakers Creed	74
28.	Yeast	76
29.	Plaited Bread	78

30.	Weights in Bakery	81
31.	Kilo-Weight	83
32.	Sourdough	87
33.	Lamination	89
34.	Healthy Bread	91
35.	Pies – Pyes	93
36.	Beer and Bread	95
37.	Pastry Work	97
38.	Confected	99
39.	Did you know (Pastry/Bakery Trivia)	101
40.	Cakes Without Borders	108
41.	Summer Baking	111
42.	Yesteryear	116
43.	The World Is a Cake	118
44.	Charles Louis Fleischmann	120
45.	The Pastry Chef	125
46.	RDT Required Dough Temperature	130
47.	Half Baked	132
48.	One Direction	134
49.	Bakers Scones	140
50.	You Know you're a Baker When…	142
51.	The Power of Pastry	147
52.	Bakery and The Foreign Legion	149
53.	Charles Joughin	154
54.	Time	156
55.	Another Book	158
56.	Fondant Icing	160
57.	Micky	163
58.	Facts and Myths of Sourdough	165
59.	Sour Dough Answered	173
60.	Excess Yolks and Whites	178
61.	Consistency	182
62.	Sponge	184

63.	Sponge and Dough	188
64.	Gluten Allergies and Intolerances	191
65.	Inactive Yeast	195
66.	Nutritional yeast	197
67.	Autolyse	198
68.	A Piece of Old Dough	200
69.	Creams (1)	202
70.	Creams (2)	204
71.	Pastry shop or Casino	207
72.	Pastry and Perfume	209
73.	No such thing as a last job!	212
74.	No-Nos – Not Yo -Yos	213
75.	Bakers Lung	217
76.	The Factor	220
77.	BP is the Key	222
78.	A Bakers Dream	225
79.	Unjustified	227
80.	Phyllo-osophy	230
81.	Bakery	234
82.	Code Of Practice	236
83.	The Bakers Prayer	238
84.	The Cycle of Life	239
85.	Bakers Tips	240
86.	In defence of sugar.	243
87.	Gateau Marjolaine	246
88.	Life's like a Donut	249
89.	The Future	250
90.	Thought Of the Day	252
91.	Xmas Baking	254
92.	Natural Sourdough Starter	256
93.	Hot Bread	258
94.	Gingerbread	260
95.	A world of Gingerbread	263

96.	Hot x Buns	265
97.	Bespoke Hot X Buns	267
98.	The Alternative HXB	269
99.	Tradition	270
100.	Cookie	271
101.	Cookie Directory	273
102.	Befriend your Oven	275
103.	Blind Baking	277
104.	The Face Book Baker	281
105.	Flat Bread	282
106.	If Life Was A Cake	284
107.	Yeast Rules	285
108.	Artisan (Magic Hands)	288
109.	Bakers Abbreviations	292
110.	Flour	294
111.	Sour Dough Answered	297
112.	To be Noted	302
113.	Fruitcake	304
114.	Scaling	307
115.	Fresh – The Bakers Deodorant	308
116.	Pastes (1)	309
117.	Pastes (2)	311
118.	Aim of the Game	314

My Baking World

From the Champs Elysée of Paris,
To Fifth Avenue in New York,
Lygon Street in Melbourne,
Bond Street of London.

Across the Atlantic, Pacific and Indian Oceans,
Through the Mediterranean and China seas,
Through the Panama Canal and across the Equator.
Round the Cape of Good Hope and the straights of Gibraltar.

Working in the Bahamas, then to Florida,
Cruising from Fort Lauderdale, then to the Caribbean.
Sydney, Perth, Canberra and Melbourne too,
The World, - A luxury cruise liner owned by its residents.

Teaching in London, demonstrating at Cordon Bleu.
Teaching in Australia, channeling ideas to book,
Pastry chef in Italian, Greek, French and Jewish Shops,
Consulting ideas, methods, formulas, recipe development.

A teacher, lecturer, demonstrator, facilitator,

Promoting education and vision for the next generation,

Historian, Speaker, promoter, researcher,

Poet, artist, author and humanitarian, and, friend of the Earth.

1. Baking Philosophy

Baking, as with all arts, sciences and religions, can pose so many questions to be studied or resolved. The term philosophy, from the Greek word "Philosophia" is a term which basically means "pursuit of knowledge for its own sake". In baking it's not necessary to question why, and probably never wise to do so either. It's a profession based on solid facts, rigorous daily routine and practice, using set formulas which have been tried and tested over time. To question, is to bring into play cross – examination, scepticism, distrust, and maybe some deceit.

Bakers are a simple breed of craftsmen/women, who take pride in their efforts, admire their end products and apply their work as a vocation rather than a job. They are a very proud bunch of skilled workers, and have none or any time for clever, questionable or smart comments which may undermine or underpin their work. As for change, it's the last thing they're contemplating, because change identifies with a break from the norm, and that can send shockwaves rocketing through their minds. Bakers in general are robotic in their approach to the workload, methodical, regimental to some degree, and precise to the closest possible millimetre. Flair and imagination are normally left to the decorators, pastry cooks, finishers and packers.

Baking is a simple craft shrouded in myths. Its coveys itself as a day-to-day essential commodity, prepared in simple conventional methods, and sold with democratic values. There is nothing painstakingly difficult to comprehend with its production, availability and consumption.

Any philosophical questions about baking are usually kept to the silent few. These could be questions which are slightly abstract in their nature and are foundational. They are questions best asked through reflection rather than experimentation. They could be questions which impede the natural thought process, ideas which go completely against the grain or visions of adopting new techniques and finally concepts which could prove to benefit both the provider and client.

The problem with philosophy is that clear answers are unattainable. Pythagoras, the most famous controversial ancient Greek philosopher (c. 570 t – c.490 BC) – possibly coined the phrase philosophy from the Greek word" philosophia" meaning "love of wisdom". This equates to the study of the most fundamental aspects of reality and value. Using philosophy can enable you to deepen your capacity and your interests by thinking more reflectively about whom you are, your place in the world and your relation to those around you. In aspects of clear thinking, it's possible to address the philosophy of baking in a completely new light.

The more the coin is flipped, the greater there are of questions to be answered. Philosophy isn't about being academic or practical for that matter, it's about questioning the norm, trying to eclipse new insights, viewpoints suggestions, etc. It's basic in its role, yet can be uplifting in its ideals, exciting in its possibilities, and enduring in its outlook. We are all philosophers to a degree, we can all have our say, we can all portray something, and we can all make our own additions, from which can make life that little bit more interesting to live.

Some are slaves of ambition or money, but others are interested in life itself. These give themselves the name philosophers, and they value the contemplation and discovery of nature beyond all other pursuits.

Pythagoras

Happy Baking!

2. Its Just a Numbers Game

"Bakery is simply a numbers game"

Its numbers in percentages, ratios, formulas, and recipes,
Numbers in timing, mixing and scaling, and weights,
Its numbers in equation, in calculation, and in quantity,
Its numbers in temperature, numbers in thermostats, in volume.
Numbers in sales, which will lead to numbers in revenue and numbers in profit.
Numbers on dates, clocks, years,
Numbers in a baker's dozen, numbers of cuts, scoring, braiding,
Numbers of turns, layers, settings and coatings,
Numbers of skills, numbers of burns, numbers of yield,
Numbers of customers, numbers of smiles and numbers of happy souls.
Numerically yours!

3. What is Baking: Baker to Baker

Top heat	Talk like a Baker
Bottom Heat	Think like a Baker
Residual Heat	Work like a Baker
Friction Heat	Prep like a Baker
Seasonal heat	Bake like a Baker
Applied heat	Measure like a Baker
Incubated heat / warmth	Process like a Baker
Increased heat	Dress like a Baker
Decreased heat	Calculate like a Baker
Coagulated heat	Furnish like a Baker
Dry Heat	Sweat / perspires like a Baker.
Moist heat	Mould like a Baker
Timed Heat	Exercise like a Baker
Combustible heat	Rise like a Baker
Gentle Heat	Toil like a Baker
Prolonged heat	Live like a Baker.
Radioactive heat	Provide like a Baker
Conduction heat	Sustain like a Baker
Convection heat	Encompass all like a baker.

Heat and Baking are aligned, products formatted and timed,

It allows for items to be consumed, and an allure perfumed,

It renders goods digestible; and the bakers work acceptable,

Overall, it provides life support, sustenance its main thought,

A profession to uphold, for all those who wish to be enrolled.

Baking Matters

4. The Baking Bug

It's hard to explain – how baking can somehow get into your blood stream trapped in each vein,

It's difficult to comprehend – how baking can somehow infatuate you, and soulmate you – like a best friend,

It's surprising how baking has the power – to supersede everything else, minute by minute, hour by hour,

And it's intoxicating how baking can suffocate – coveting your thought processes without causing you to frustrate.

If baking is in your blood – it's in your blood, and nothing can transcend you from the so-called baking club,

If baking governs your life – and by that we mean mind, body, soul, in whatever capacity, without stress or strife,

If baking is everything to you – whether it's early morning, late evening, or weekends when that need starts to brew,

Then welcome to the "Baking bug " – where every day becomes another cake, recipe and conquest – including cakes that are baked in a mug.

5. Bakers Hands

What are Bakers hands – If not a gift from God!
What do they portray – aged, worn by a road well-trod?
These are the carpus which furnish our daily bread,
These are the crucibles, from which the masses are fed.

Bakers' hands are like asbestos, forged and well endured,
Bakers' hands are manual, cognitive and diligently spurred,
These working tools akin to the best thermometers around,
These labour intensive, practical aids, well and truly ground.

Bakers' hands can mould, braid and roll concentrical circles,
Bakers' hands can align, measure and scoop recipe referrals,
These hands can deposit, scrape, dust, sheet, wipe and fold,
These hands can line and arrange doughs pressed and rolled.

Bakers' hands can have Burns, Scalds, Cuts and floured nails,
Bakers' hands can be chapped, swollen, oiled as machinery fails,
These hands are gentle when when moulding softer doughs,
These hands don't overhandle, overwork, or undermine tastes.

Bakers' hands twist knots, form bagels, shape and roll scrolls,
Bakers' hands scale, divide, stretch, and give the ciabatta folds,
These hands are credited with giving life to the yeasted matter,
These hands, that enrich our lives with daily doughs and batter.

Bakers' hands can crimp, mould, seal, scrape and spread,
Bakers' hands can punch, knockback, de-gas our daily bread,
These hand which can be protected by flannel oven mitts,
These hands that roll and form those elongated French sticks.

Bakers' hands engage and for this we are so truly blessed,
Bakers' hands are seemingly unsung, not knowingly addressed,
These hands that we dismiss, indebted for each day,
These Bakers hands need validation, and praise without delay.

6. The Bakers Consensus

Your Baked goods shouldn't look anaemic or carbonised,
Your croissant and Danish should reflect an air of flakiness,
Your puff pastry should be risen 4-5-fold its unbaked height,
Your Baked muffins should resemble a mushroom topping,
    General Agreement!!!!

Your Buttercream should contain a minimum of 17% Butter,
Your doughnuts should be fried for 4 minutes at 180C,
    (2 mins each side)
Your choux pastry should be baked – but must also be dried out,
Your Sweet pastry / shortbread should be short, tender and fragile,
    Common consent!!!!

Your Natural starter is fed, nurtured and protected daily,
Your Fresh cream goods are regulated, replenished, rotated, chilled,
Your fondant work is correctly tempered, set and not crystallised,
Your glazes and ganache, clear, clean, smooth, set and shiny,
    Like mindedness!!!!!

Your oven is allowed to dictate the daily workflow,
Your work is prioritised by working 1-3 days in advance,
Your fridge and freezer temperatures are monitored daily,
Your appliances cleaned, maintained, serviced, regulated,
    A Concurrence!!!!

Your suppliers greeted with curtesy, respect, acknowledgment,
Your cleanings schedule implemented, adhered too, controlled,
Your stance, professional, proficient and pro-active,
Your work ethic, reflective, responsible and rewarding.
    Adopted – without a vote!!!

7. Bread

(The currency of humanity)

Loaves, flat breads, sticks, rolls,
Accommodate the world more than gold,
Floured, seeded, scored or plain.
Trusted flavours from harvested grain.

Shaped, braided, twisted and knotted,
Tinned, moulded, batched or clay potted,
They all require the same time and devotion,
To create a finish that aids sales and promotion.

Whether sour, sprouted, grained or malted,
All breads require flavour, and to be evenly salted,
Correct fermentation to form texture, aid digestion,
With time and temperature included, to aid aeration.

Doughs prepped from wheat, rye, wholemeal or spelt,
With varying flours such as oat or maize from the Corn Belt,
Barley, Amaranth, Triticale, and Gluten free also included,
Teff, Quinoa, Buckwheat and Atta flour not to be excluded.

Semolina or sharps used to aid moulding and finishing,
Seeds and grains added to complete the distinguishing,
Flours for dusting, pastes for tiger bread, glazes for buns,
Embracing man's staple food to all creeds and all tongues.

8. Bread

Whole meal Vienna

Stone baked whole meal Vienna

Vienna,

Swiss Vienna

Split Vienna

Floured Vienna

Rye Vienna sourdough

Quinoa Linseed Vienna,

Olive and Basil Vienna,

Low GI 7 Seeds & Grains Vienna

Stone baked Soy and Linseed

Multi Grain Loaf

Cobs,

Devon,

Wheat germ loaf,

Stone baked sourdough

Pastadura, (dense heavy white loaf)

Pane di Casa loaf – (Crusty loaf with a soft interior)

Stone baked Pane de Casa

Rye Pane di Casa

Stone-ground wholegrain loaf – (wheat and rye)

Seed and Sprout loaf – (sprouted wheat and buckwheat)

Vollkorn loaf (Rye spelt and rye sprouts)

Whole meal ciabatta,

Ciabatta,

Foccacia,

Panini

Plain rye,

Farmer's rye,

Caraway rye,

Sunflower rye,

Whole meal rye sour

Bavarian rye,

Rye whole meal,

Walnut rye,

New York Rye,

Sultana /Raisin Rye

Light Rye Boulle (Cob)

Light Rye Sourdough,

Turkish bread.

Afghan bread (garlic and herbs)

Sour sticks,

Fruit challa

Plain challa

Soy linseed bread

Pipe loaf

Rustic

Walnut rustic

Spelt loaf

Spelt Sourdough

Spelt Bloomer

White Spelt and Caraway loaf

Olive bread

Farmhouse cottage loaf

Bloomer

Seeded Bloomer

Poppy seed Bloomer

Roast pumpkin Bloomer,

Twist,

Milk Bread loaves

Tiger Bread

French sticks

Seeded French sticks

Baguettes

Demi – Baguettes

Ficelle sticks

Bagels

Banh-mi rolls

Tuscany bread (no salt)

Granary bread

Stone sour dough loaf

Sour dough Vine fruit dough

Sourdough Cob,

Bread

Hi-Tin

Hi-Fibre

Chubb Block

Square tin block,

Harvest Grain,

Corn Tin,

Organic white casalinga loaf

Fig, Apricot, Sultana Loaf,

Date and nut loaf,

Brioche Burger Bun /sliders,

Knotted rolls,

Seeded Rolls,

Foccacia rolls

Turkish rolls,

Dinner Rolls,

Finger Rolls,

Rye currant and walnut Rolls,

Wheat sheaf display bread

Pumpkin seeded loaf (Tin or Freeform Vienna)

Brioche

Pretzels

Bagels

Seeded Bagels (Sesame)

7seed Hi -Fibre low Gi rolls

Soft Damper rolls

White Hi -Fibre Low Gi rolls

9. The Bakehouse

Bakeries are not meant to be sterile, clinical, polished meticulous environments or venues.

They are the opposite with wooden tables, flour dusted surfaces, intoxicating baking fumes, musty odors from doughs, yeasts and fat, and the air ladened with the warmth of fermentation and baking. Bakeries are meant to be semi-murky -not dirty or unclean – but like a living incubator which retains yeast spores, where the smell of fermentation from old dough, sponges, ferments, starters, and flour dust can be prevalent.

Wooden tables –Why?

Because they harbour bacteria from the previous doughs – give good molding friction – are always an ambient temperature – perfect for breadmaking – despite health and safety officers denouncing them since they are unhygienic. Wooden tables connect us with the land, the soil, the nature of our being. They are practical, they are bio – degradable, they give comfort, they connect us to Mother Earth. There is no better surface to work on with bread than wood. That's why many bakers who have unfortunately been given notice to change their working surfaces where environmental rules have been stringent – have resolved to obtaining a metal covering surface over the top of wood – which is able to be removed and replaced when and where necessary.

Tough times – tough measures!

Bread troughs – dough troughs – Petrin, were always used for breadmaking for centuries –and so were dough proving drawers under wooden bakers' benches –to maintain the dough and its temperature, to get the best fermentation and development. Baking isn't a new Instagram craze or a Tik – Tok video entertainment hub – it's been around for centuries. Baking history is more entrenched in civilization than the creation of alcohol, so for it to be redesigned or somehow reformatted based on red tape over-analyzing – is both ignorant and foolhardy.

Bakery is steeped in time – steeped in tradition, and like farming doesn't warm to change. old systems – old methods – are clung on to with validity and clear consciousness. Bakers know what works, what doesn't, how the seasons affect workload, how environmental issues have always been at the forefront of their minds. Without grains, flours, seeds, dairy, they are nowhere. They don't need or require rhetoric from so-called activists, green army, or modern-day earth gurus. They need compliance, preferably subsidies from the government, appreciation for their craft/skills, a fair go, an opportunity to be part of the community, an understanding from the public, and preferably a higher social status than what exists today.

Clean, sanitised, spotless bakeries just become soulless. They relate to car showrooms – void of any emotional ties, any connection, any real purpose. Bakeries should be a life – source and treated as such. What is bread but man's /person's staple food? They are the engine room of sustenance, the workhouse of mankind. The products are the most basic of foodstuff – a necessity more so than a yearning -a life source. It's the one product which binds all sunder, all creeds, all cultures.

Bread in all its guises, stigmatises simplicity, the uncomplexity of living, the "manna" of life. It's a humble product, never overriding or demanding, never stealing the limelight, or overshadowing its accompaniments. It carries, it holds, wraps, protects, builds, encompasses – but it never portrays itself for more than what it is. Bread is simply Bread produced by Bakers.

Quote – "Simplicity is the ultimate sophistication."

10. Baking Truths

Baking is simply a means to an end. Only on marrying it with a business, does it become a profession. Otherwise, it remains simply a form of entertainment, achievement, or may be a provision for others, be it family or friends, a hobby or pastime, or some form of therapeutic enjoyment.

Baking unfortunately doesn't levitate you to great wealth and stardom, unless you're one of the chosen few, who just happen to be in the right place at the right time, with supposedly the right connections and the right face. Even then you may prosper – but wealth which equals money and time – is questionable. Yes, there are the minority who have succeeded in gaining that – but they're few and far between.

What commercial baking will do is sap you of your energy, deprive you of your normal sleeping patterns, delude you of having any status, and expect you to work unsociable hours and public holidays, with little remuneration and without penalty or award rates. You'll be excluded from certain social circles due to your working hours, acquire baker's hands, breath in flour dust to your lungs, become pale and anaemic and withdrawn looking, grow tired legs, and ask yourself a multitude of times what are you doing in life exactly. The graveyard shift has few friends, can be a lonely solitary place, if not for a radio or some form of audio entertainment.

Summer can be hot, winter cold. You'll feel exploited at times by the system, wages, and hours. Being subservient to the cause is your response to retaining some forms of loyalty to the job, some allegiance with baking bread and a self-guarantee that you are playing your role in society to sustaining and participating to make a better World.

All sounds too bad? Well, the upside to the coin is that Baking can fill many voids in people's lives. Baking is like gardening – it can add value to your life – give you a different perspective – humble you – make you realise that life isn't that bad – the World isn't such a corrupt place. It can put you back in tune with Earths biorhythms' and make you appreciate the simple basic factors of life. Baking is meant to be therapeutic, and an honourable profession – if not a vocation – but it's a marriage of physical labour, and commitment, early hours – and it is surprising how many people can turn to it in later life, as well as offenders in prison, who see it as a way to re -communicate with themselves and the outside world, and give themselves some form of dignity, self-worth and self-belief to carry on in society. You could call it a form of rehabilitation.

All in all, baking is something that you simply do – no questions asked.

Like it or loathe it, dream of it or despair it, connect with it or disengage from it, the choice is yours. It's not an easy profession, it never has been, and it never will be. As the old saying goes – "work doesn't stop – only people stop", which is worth noting.

Baking is what you make baking. Baking won't give you the answers to life; neither will it provide physical, mental or emotional assistance, but it will however give you that purpose in life.

With purpose, life makes sense, like the jigsaw of life, by putting it all together; the clear picture will begin to show clarity to your life, give it a meaning, give it worth, self-respect, honour, commitment, and most important the answers to yourself.

Baking is democratic; it's a form of libertarianism, it's the need within the deed, it's like the running water from the tap. If it ceased to be, there would be panic, uproar, fear, and total civil unrest. That's how important it is, regardless of the everyday apathy to its being. The attitude of its just a cheap basic commodity, take it or leave it, will continue, and prices will always demean its value.

But, like everything in life, people only value things once in demise or maybe simply unavailable. In the meantime, the show must go on, the masses need to be fed, hunger dissipated, farmers and millers kept smiling.

Bread can be gold.

11. The Laws and Lores of Bakery

Laws are basically the system of rules which a particular country or community recognises as regulating the actions of its members and which it may enforce. The law serves many purposes and functions in society.

Four principal purposes and functions are, establishing standards, maintaining order, resolving disputes, and protecting liberties and rights.

In Baking as in any other matter, there are laws perpetuating to certain products, certain disciplines, certain practices, certain weights and measures, labelling, legislations, taxes, and employment.

In contrast, Lores are defined as the body of knowledge, especially of a traditional, anecdotal, or popular nature on a particular subject. This pertains to tradition, knowledge, stories, and cultural beliefs.

In France National law dictates that French bread should contain only flour, yeast, salt and water. The baguette (French stick) became the iconic symbol of French bread and France in the 20th Century when a law was passed in 1920 banning bakers from starting work before 4 am and no later than 10 pm, which made it difficult for them to have fresh bread for the morning, so they made the fast-baking baguette as a solution. Today there are strict guidelines to the standard baguette, e.g., size, diameter, length and a weight of 250 g to 300gms.

According to the French bread law of 1993, known as the "decret pain", it is deemed perfectly natural / legitimate for bakers to add yeast to natural starter bread (Pain au Levain) if they stick to the strict guidelines of not adding more than 2grams per Kilo of flour.

Because bread is such an integral part of French life, culture and food, and expectations are so high, it's estimated that around ten million baguettes are sold each year in France. That's why Bakers in France are seen as part of the life force of the country, an essential service, as important as any high-flying corporative management, and on par with all the high profile academic, medical, and financial Professionals.

Up until 2014, the law in France stated that Bakers could not vacate at the same time during the summer month holiday period. This law was upturned.

In Germany, the title of master baker is a requirement for opening a bakery of your own. To obtain entry to the National Master Bakers Academy, the law states that three years of education and experience are obtained in a bakery, plus an examination, and as well as some years of experience as a baker prior to being granted entry. Bakery in Germany is one of the professions which are subject to a "Meisterpflicht" – or you have been through the German apprentice training system to "Meister" (Foreman-Master Craftsman/woman).

By following this format, they uphold the stringent requirements of quality and craft, thus enabling the profession to be respected and admired.

Vollkornbot (whole grain bread) in Germany is protected by a law. It states that it is mandatory that vollkornbrot bread must have a whole grain flour content of 90%. This bread is of the dark brown and Rye flour, which is regarded as that off the healthy variety. Most whole grain breads account under the same heading, which are commonly eaten in the evening in Germany with cheese and cold meats.

In Italy the home of the Panettone Cakes, there are also laws and regulations governing its procedure and make up. The law stipulates that certain yeasts must be used in the production of the seasonal Milanese panettone Cake, and these are the traditional methods of using beer yeast / brewer's yeast, as opposed to bread making yeasts. This law was implemented to safeguard the traditional methods of an industry which produces on average, 170 million panetonne and Pandora cakes annually, at an estimated value of 859 million US dollars, 579 million euros, 416 million pounds.

At one time Panettone was a specialty product, calling for higher prices. However, fierce domestic competition at the end of World War two commoditised the product and making it affordable for everyone. Furthermore, Italian ex-pats to Argentina and Brazil brought their love of Panettone to Central and South America where it became popular and spawned a new industry.

Thus, the minister of Agriculture in Italy proposed a law which was put forward to the European union and world trade organization to restrict the name Panettone to only Italian made cakes, and to better ensure customers understand the difference authenticity makes and to protect domestic bakers. These laws are like current Italian laws governing wine, cheese, and chacuterie. For example, only parmesan cheese produced in Italy, can be called Parmesan cheese.

This then states that imported Panettone highlights the Italian law that makes the effective claim that it is made using traditional methods, using the traditional ingredients, especially beer yeast.

These laws are for all Panettone for the domestic market within Italy, and the law is not statuary for exported Panettone. Only butter and beer yeast Panetonne can be made destined for Italian households. As such, Italians feel that Panetonne originating from Latin America or exported to other countries should be considered "Panetonne-like" or "Italian style" – but not authentic.

The classic panetonne is governed by the minister of Productive Activities, which sets a series of elements that set it apart to other styles and shapes and flavours to other types of made panetonne cake. These are dough, crust, shape, and above all ingredients.

These ingredients are set by law. The classic Panetonne should contain butter (not less than 16%), candied citrus peel, sugar, wheat flour, eggs, (minimum 4% egg yolk), salt, leaven. If desired you can add honey, milk, and dairy products, cocoa, malt, spices, other yeast (not more than 1%) preservatives such as potassium sorbate, and sorbic acid.

The selling of underweight bread was once a punishable crime in yesteryear. In the city of London, the offence for selling bread below the legal minimum weight was to be dragged through the city with the offending loaf around the person's neck. The second offence was to be put in the pillory (the stretch neck) for an hour, which allowed the public to throw whatever they liked at the offenders, and some items could be near lethal. Third offence the baker's oven was pulled down, thus ending the persons business, and unless someone bailed them out, they would end up in the poor house.

Today the law is still as stringent if not more. Fines are extremely high when underweight bread is sold to customers. Bread man's most basic staple foodstuff – and therefore to deceive the public by profiteering with the staff of life – is inexcusable.

The term a baker's dozen is a term synonymous with the number 13 in place of 12. The history behind this was simple – for bakers to inadvertently sell underweight bread – they would give an extra roll or loaf thrown in to avoid unpleasant punishment. The written phase was first recorded in 1599, but for centuries bakers routinely gave one or two extra loaves or buns for the price of a dozen. Good business practice/ marketing from the baker's point of view – but basically it was their safety net to avoid breaking the law of the land.

In other countries, history records that punishment was even more severe. For example, in Vienna – bakers caught selling underweight bread were put in a cage that was plunged in the river several times, and in Turkey a bad baker would be stretched out on his own kneading table and the "bastinado" – foot beating with a stick was administered.

The most public and painful punishment was in ancient Egypt, where an offending baker could be nailed by the ear to the door of his shop. Probably the most humiliating of all the punishments as his customers could also throw in more abuse and vile extremities.

Today, weights and measures governed by the law will come down heavy on any offending participant if failure to comply with trading standards. This could involve and include a fine / or imprisonment. (Trading standards powers, enforcement and penalties)

There is a simple three rule process that must be complied with, relating to the permitted underweight loaves. It's a legal requirement for checks to be carried out on baked loaves before they are offered for sale to ensure they pass the three-rule process. Except for wrapped bread, a record of the checks need not be kept – however it's a good idea to show that your baking process is being controlled to produce bread of the required weight. This process is normally geared toward large manufacturers rather than the small retail shop baker – however the law remains the same, and the regulations still play importance as how and in what manner bread is weighted, scaled, baked and sold.

Non – Packaged loaves are not required to be sold by weight.

The Three Rules

1. The average weight of a baked batch of a type of bread must not be less than the Qn
2. Approximately no more than one in 40 loaves of the baked batch may have a negative error greater than the tolerable negative error E) – that is weigh less than Qn minus TNE.
3. None of the loaves in the baked batch may have a negative error greater than twice the TNE – that is weigh less than Qn minus 2TNE.

Asking for Fresh Yeast

It was expected anyone walking into a baker requiring some fresh yeast, was obligingly served with a small quantity for home baking. This was never an actual written law, but an excepted law, that fresh yeast was given free with no cost as it is basically the bacteria required to produce a form of edible bread in the home. Supermarkets where bread was baked on site, also were expected to hand over fresh yeast on request – no charge – as again this being staple food requirements on a humanitarian basis.

Today with many bakers using instant dried yeast and it being readily available on supermarket shelves – with extended shelf life, this practice is rarely seen these days, Also the vast array of breads on sale from corner shops to service stations and 24-hour supermarkets, has basically diminished and practically made obsolete this request.

12. Rules of Engagement

There exist two types of dough making – Time and No time doughs.

The two most essential elements in Bakery are – Time and Temperature.

The fifth ingredient in breadmaking is the most important – "Time" – following Flour, Water, Yeast, and Salt.

No time doughs require increased yeast levels, accelerators such as bread improvers, and in some cases a small percentage of added sugar.

There are three main methods of dough making, Straight dough, Ferment and dough, Sponge and Dough. (Salt delayed can be incorporated into either of these)

Sour dough should epitomise three things – Purity, crust, flavour.

Sour doughs need time – and a fermentation period of 12-18-36 hours allow for enzyme breakdown of the starches, and full flavour and acidic notes to aspire.

Natural starter, mothers, bread cultures encapsulate the same meaning. These need to be maintained daily – or at least every other day.

Starters can be wheat, whole meal, or rye – depending on product and manufacturer. The starter is your driving force of your bread – hence duty of care, feed and timing are essential.

Ciabatta, Focaccia doughs and Turkish bread require high hydration levels – ranging from 70-90% water with the addition of oil -either olive oil or a blend of olive and vegetable oils.

Ciabatta dough can be made with strong flour or plain flour, and even a mixture of the two – like an all-purpose flour – if a crisper ciabatta is required. Ciabatta (slipper bread) is exceptional bread for sandwich Panini, and focaccia is also good for lunch rolls and garnished flat breads. Excess flour is always used when working Ciabatta dough.

Focaccia dough can be worked with olive oil or semolina pending on the Bakers requirements. It is normally dimpled out with olive oil or placed on a baking sheet with semolina underneath and again dimpled out with hands spread eagle. It is a useful base for pizza rounds and trays and can also be molded into a round for focaccia rolls. Use olive oil and thyme and sundried tomatoes as a topping for the rolls or leave plain for a crisper surface.

Ciabattini are small square rolls made with Ciabatta dough and are excellent for small sandwiches with a crisp crust. Ciabatta dough is normally heavily floured as opposed to Focaccia which are dimpled with olive oil before garnishing or left plain.

Turkish breads can be sprayed with water or brushed with milk before sprinkled with a mixture of sesame seeds and nigella seed – ratio three sesame to one nigella. This is an exceptional sandwich bread for breakfast rolls and lunchtime sandwiches.

Sharps, semolina, polenta, and rice cones, prevent doughs from adhering to and assist in sliding.

Soda breads are chemically aerated – therefore needing cultured buttermilk, yoghurt, or acidic sour milk to counteract the after taste of baking powder or bicarbonate of soda.

Toscana loaves In Italy are traditionally non – salted – due to the porchetta or highly seasoned meat sauces they accompany – and /or the olives added from brine.

However – for Bakers to sell Toscana Bread in other countries – it is common to produce a bread with a low salt addition. Many Bakeries opt for lower salt than completely omitting it all together.

Bloomers, Vienna, and cobs traditionally are all scored accordingly – 4 diagonal cuts for Vienna, 7-13 diagonal cuts for a bloomer loaf, three Criss – cross cuts for a cob. A Coburg / sour Coburg is a Cob – baked on a tray – not a tin with a deep cross on the top.

A Farmhouse loaf traditionally is double stacked, welded together by pushing a rod or finger through the centre cavity of the two pieces of dough, then floured, and scored around the sides, but more recently is baked in a bread tin, floured, and scored with a straight line down the centre.

Rye Bread is normally produced with a combination of either light rye flour or dark rye flour with the addition of wheat flour. This combination can be 60/40 – 70/30 -or 100% Rye flour in the case of Pumpernickel bread or pure dark rye loaves.

Rye sour dough loaves are normally produced with a wry starter which can benefit from the use of beer as part of its feed. The sour dough 100% Rye loaf needs 24 hours resting after baking before being sold to the public to allow the proteose gluten to condition itself for consumption.

Rye loaves are commonly sold with the additions of soy, carraway seeds, linseed, sunflower, sultanas, or pumpkin to vary and modify the loaves. Other loaves include Dark Rye Sunflower sour dough, Dark Rye Sandwich fruit and muesli loaf, Country grain and organic Rye spelt and sprouted grains, 12 grain and seeds loaf sour Rye grain, Sour linseed and sourdough organic Rye, Sauerkraut Rye Bread, Rye and olive loaf, and Rye and Anise loaf.

Whole meal loaves are normally sold pure 100% whole meal – or they are a blend of whole meal and wheat flour on a ratio of 50/50 – 70/30 – 90/10. These loaves can also be flavoured and enhanced using other flours – to offer more interesting taste and texture – such as Whole meal and Rye sandwich loaf.

The whole meal, whole wheat and whole grain are different forms of the same thing.

Wheat germ bread has an added 25% wheat germ added to the flour which lowers the gluten content of the dough. Honey and milk can be included to wheat germ breads and offer a more mellow texture and taste, plus increasing the nutritional value of the bread from the germ.

Multi – Grain breads can compose of various seeds and grains. Seven seeded loaves are a popular variety of these types of breads – however then is no set rule or distinction between the additions and varieties used. Some multi – grain loaves can be processed with 12 various grains and because of this high volume, a little sweetness is added to the dough in the form of honey, to counteract the bitterness from the grains.

It is widespread practice to roll and coat the doughs with seeds before pacing onto baking trays or into tins.

Sourdough multi – grain – whole meal multi – grain and Rye multi grain are all popular varieties of the low Gi – and high fiber candidates.

Seeds include sunflower, chia, poppy, sesame, pumpkin, flax, linseed, and quinoa.

Kibbled wheat and grains can also be included.

Challah are normally braided with four strands of dough – but can also be woven with up to 12 strands. The weaving motion is used for whatever number of strands, and goes from Left to right, 2nd to the top and 1st to the middle – and then right to left repeated, until the strands are completely woven.

This method of weaving can apply to any number of strands.

Bilka are individual braided rolls – either plain or seeded and in some cases have the addition of raisins or topped as a streusel Bilka.

These breads are commonly prepared and sold on Friday before sunset – as part of the Jewish Sabbath on the Saturday. They can be plain, seeded and can even be shaped round as a crown.

Pane di Casa loaves – (Italian House Bread) should traditionally be stone baked – thus encouraging good crust formation. They can be seeded if required – and made into individual shapes and portions. It is favourable to use some starter – sourdough discard or pre-ferment in these loaves to obtain good volume, bloom, and correct crust.

Normally they are unseeded. Pane Di Casa has a denser crumb with a crunchy crust due to the semolina flour, opposed to sourdough which has a chewy crust and more open texture.

Fruit loaves can be produced with either a straight dough – ferment and dough – sponge and dough or a Sour dough fruit loaf. Fruit content can differ from 30% up to 70% depending on recipe formula and manufacturer. Normally raisins/ sultanas/ dried figs/ dried apricots / dates – plus the use of dried cherries or cranberries can be added too.

Either hand moulded or baked in a tin – these loaves can be rolled and coated in sesame seeds before being placed in the tin or on to the baking tray. If the left plain the top surface can be glazed with sugar syrup on removing the oven.

Milk Breads are best produced with scalded full cream milk, this decreasing the lactose affecting the yeast activity. Fats are also normally added to these types of doughs, and produce a whiter, more tender, softer eating product, which is especially good for individual rolls and fingers. It is also useful for bridge rolls – which are normally consumed at cocktail parties and events.

This type of dough is also exceptionally good for producing bread wraps for sandwich production.

Brioche doughs are exclusively made for high grade products – due to the fact it contains a high percentage of butter – and this will occur a high-cost factor. Products made from this dough can include buns, donuts, scrolls and many savoury products encased in a soft eating dough. The paste has a dual action of being able to accommodate both sweet and savoury.

Brioche can flavour accordingly either with chopped chives for savoury rolls, rolled out as a paste to cover savoury fillings such as sausage or salmon, or it can be flavoured with brandy and encase sweet custard for a pastry or dessert.

Fried Bread – known as Fricassee –heralds from Tunisia but is popular in middle eastern counties as well. It's a simple dough produced with an exceedingly small percentage of sugar – 25grams per Kilo of flour- and then the remaining ingredients as for a donut dough – including some egg. After fermentation, it is scaled and shaped into a small oval bun, proved and then deep-fried like a donut. Its garnishes and fillings include a variety of meat, fish, and salads.

Bun doughs are primarily a bread dough – enriched with sugar, eggs, fats, flavouring and milk. They should always be tender eating and not tough, due to the high fat content from the milk, yolks from the eggs and fat. They can be produced in a variety of ways and garnishes, fillings, shapes, and finishing's and are best prepared from a ferment and dough or a sponge and dough which will provide better volume and flavour.

They can be baked, deep fried, air fried and incorporated into other doughs such as scones and Danish pastry.

Hot cross buns are the most common of all bun dough goods, incorporating mixed dried fruits, orange peel, brown and white sugars, and heavily spiced. Because they are a seasonal product – they should be prepared accordingly using high quality ingredients and careful due diligent input. The flavour and colour will benefit also from replacing some of the wheat flour with a small percentage of rye and wholemeal flour.

Viennoiserie – Croissant, Danish, and certain Puff paste products, are commonly known as morning goods. Viennoiserie paste should contain butter – however many companies use modified fats using butter, and vegetable fats combined, or certain laminating margarines. Butter is superfluous in taste and should always be the first option or call to. Butter croissants should be butter croissant – Danish will taste better without any after mouth feel from hydrogenated fats – and the same applies to puff pastry goods. The ratio of fat for laminating should be approximately 30% minimum or more if so desired. The temperature of the fat should be around 16C to assist with laminating. The price of butter will be the determining factor.

It is more advisable to commence laminated doughs a day in advance. Aim for 24 hours with the preparation of the dough/detrempe and formulation of fat preparation. This allows for easier handling of the paste and more controllability.

French sticks or baguettes are always an in-house requirement. Demi – Baguettes or small French sticks (Ficelle) are a bonus to have on sale. There are various varieties of these products mostly based on their manufacture – their finish – their location and their method of production. This can be a commercially prepared straight dough or a natural fermented sour dough or a delayed salt dough to enable less gluten development. Size is determined by weight – but the general rule is 250 – 300 grams in weight – and 55-65 cm long. The scoring normally requires 5 cuts – but this can be increased or decreased pending on the manufacturer.

Their finish can be commercial, rustic floured, and their interior multi grain or whole meal.

Banh -Mi rolls are a Vietnamese style sandwich roll which are universally popular. They are a byproduct of the commercial French sticks and are popular in sandwich bars and take-away fooderies. They comprise of small rolls produced from a straight dough which comprises of flour, sugar, salt, soya flour, milk powder, improver, butter, and water and are scaled at 130grams,

They are best baked in a "Revent Model" oven, or a fan assisted convector oven with plenty of steam to create a thin crispy exterior. The characteristics should be crisp with a soft interior. Many Vietnamese will remove the inside of the roll – rejecting the starchy interior – and replacing it by adding more filling.

Flavoured Breads are breads produced using a puree of vegetables such as pumpkins or sweet potato purees, as well as olive breads, walnut breads, cheese breads, herb flavoured breads such as rosemary and olive oil.

Quinoa and walnut sourdough can also be included as flavoured Breads, Cracked Buckwheat and Pepita Bread, Onion Bread, Tahini, linseed and sesame Bread, sunflower and Barley Bread, whole meal honey and Oat bran Bread, Mushroom Bread, Tomato and cracked black pepper Bread and Blue cheese and fresh Herb Bread.

Other breads include Herbed Polenta bread, Buttermilk Bread, Cheddar and green olive bread, Semolina Bread, Cheddar Beer Bread, Basil and Garlic Bread, Cornmeal pepper Bread, Sour cream and onion Bread, Herbed pumpkin bread, Butternut squash bread, whole wheat, onion, and dill bread.

Potato Bread has the addition of mashed, pureed potato or dried potato flour or flakes – which replaces a percentage of the wheat flour. Irish farls are a common early type of potato bread which were cooked on gridles or a frying pan. They can include a variety of flavours such as grated zucchini / courgettes, spinach, bacon, fresh herbs, cheese, and onion, and even cinnamon and sugar. The potato also acts as a leavening agent which allows for less yeast or in some cases – no yeast.

Potato loaves offer a much softer meal, denser texture, very white, and with a slightly sweeter flavour – which is excellent for sandwiches and toasting. These loaves were quite common during the Second World War period, when there was extreme rationing of basic foodstuffs.

Banana Bread is a chemically aerated loaf consisiting of broken-down banana, eggs, flour, sugars, fats, eggs, spices, and flavouring. Although common as a breakfast item – either toasted or untoasted – its high sugar content merges it more towards an American style muffin breakfast cake. It can include the addition of walnuts, and frozen or dried blueberries, and other garnishing's to make it more appealing and varied.

Almond Bread is produced from meringue with the addition of flour and lightly toasted whole natural almonds. It's baked in cake tins before being sliced and then re-toasted in the oven until crisp and coloured. It's usually served as an accompaniment to coffee.

It consists of fresh egg white, caster sugar, plain soft flour, and whole natural almonds.

Bagels and Pretzels are common amongst many bakeries, especially bagels in kosher bakeries and pretzels because they are the Germanic symbol of bakery. Bagels in kosher bakeries are not allowed to use milk or milk powder in the dough -as meat and milk must remain separate – but otherwise the milk powder will give good crust formation when baking.

Bagels are primarily boiled before baking – but recently this has been replaced by extra steam injection in the oven when initially baking. The excess steam or boiling provides good crisp, crust, and sheen formation which is symbolic of a bagel. Seeding after boiling also adds flavour texture and overall appearance to add to customers preferences and requirements.

In practice, Bagels can be rolled by hand or produced by tabletop bagel depositor machines. They provide excellent sandwich rolls allowing for a variety of fillings either toasted or untoasted.

Pretzels are uniquely represented by their shape, which is a symmetrical form of dough intertwined and then twisted back on itself – known as a loop or pretzel bow. The three holes in the pretzel shape have an ancient religious meaning symbolizing the Father, the Son, and the Holy spirit – although in German bakeries it is seen as a symbol of Good Luck, Prosperity, and Spiritual fulfillment.

The shaped pretzel is passed through a solution of boiling Lye – (Wearing goggles and gloves, as the solution is Costic and could burn) and it is this which gives the pretzel its traditional skin, colour and flavour, through what is known as the Maillard reaction. They are immediately sprinkled with rock salt / sea salt.

They are normally cut /slashed to a depth of one centimeter in the thick part at the top back prior to baking.

Kosher baking requires an understanding of Jewish dietary laws – also known as Kashrut. This regulates which foods can be eaten, how they are prepared and how they are combined.

The main rules in baking are no mixing of dairy and meat products, no mixing of utensils, table, and ovens for meat and dairy products. Normally utensils are marked M for milk and P for pareve if working in a kosher Bakery. If non – kosher these rules do not apply.

Strict governing by the Rabbi and Shomer govern the abidance of these set procedures and can if so required interrupt production and sales if not adhered to and certification.

Other basic rules in Kosher baking are, keeping a piece of dough made from each Batch for the Rabbi,

No Baking after Sunset on the Friday, as Saturday is the Sabbath.

No Bread thrown away,

Use of kosher products.

Halal Baking is like Kosher baking in the sense it must comply with a set of rules. It must go through a mandatory certification process to ascertain Halal standards.

No items can be prepared or consumed which contain any traces of pork, alcohol, carnivorous meat, birds of prey or insects. However, meat and poultry can be permitted in the diet if they follow the rule of the animal must be alive and blessed in the name of Allah, the Islamic God, before being slaughtered.

Hygiene is a crucial factor, and items such as meat-based gelatine are not allowed. If Halal products are to be produced in an everyday commercial bakery – then a separate area should be allocated for this preparation.

All products baked must identify with halal markings for customers' notification.

There are a variety of grains, seeds and flours on the marketplace, and bread does not simply need to be the so-called cotton wool variety, bland, and uninteresting.

Bread has been formatted for years and has included Barley, Rye, Buckwheat, Millet, Sorghum, Durum and semolina, Soy, Amaranth, Atta, Chickpea, Rice flour, Teff, Emmer, Fava, Lupin, Potato and Quinoa.

As Bakers, our duty is to provide a product that is both nutritious, healthy, interesting, digestible, fit for human consumption and most importantly, bread that is memorable and flavorsome.

13. Cake

Will you customise, personalise, and personify my cake,
    Will you make it unique, different, a complete contrast from the everyday bake?
    Try to remember I'm different; I'm not like the rest,
    I'm me, my own entity; I want uniqueness to be my personal quest.

Welcome to "me-cake", if you know what I mean,
    Where the customer thinks their apart and something unusual to be seen,
    Here individuality, non-contemporary, is the order of the day.
    Like taking a mobile selfie, -except here, it's their cake that's on display.

For them an individual cake is not about size or portion control,
    It's not about the height, width, weight or any other goal,
    Here it's about narcissism, the limelight deprivation syndrome, me, me, me,
    What represents them, their being, their existence, their uncompromising plea?

Do I look the same as everyone else, they cry?
    Do I represent fodder, the norm, the masses or simply that another guy?

Don't I deserve what I want, need and like, -Can't I have it all, they sigh,

Isn't it my life, my choice, my decision, my right – without the questioning why.

It's good to be different, unusual, stand out, a change from the so called mundane,

But were talking about a cake here, that's ephemeral and can't gather such fame,

What is required here is reality, feet on the ground, some sense of normality.

For a product that might not even make the end of day, as around about possibility.

Why inflict this pain and necessity on something as pure and simple as a cake,

When the whole purpose of this object, is to communicate and share for all sake,

A cake was intended to eat, nurture sweet cravings, embody family and friends,

It's a symbol of joy, celebrations, happiness and smiles – not individualistic trends.

Some may argue that the whole purpose of cake is to show individualism and creativity,

Some may state that it's important to show difference and satisfy the customers' liberty,

Others may claim the importance of "break away", from so called perceived notions,

And others will utilise a cake to make or form statements, from whatever their concoctions.

Where do you draw the line, I hear you say?

What is wrong and what is right, in this so-called modern-day cake convey,

How do we re-adjust the balance for bakers/pastry cooks to put clarity to this demand?

It can only really boil down to the pricing – of which we will have to make our own stand.

Some customers will accept, some will disagree,

Some will be happy; others will want to barter, over what they see as an excessive fee,

But if this whole episode of so called modern political cake correctness is not addressed,

Then we could end up in an industry which is governed by the so called "My cake Celebs".

14. SPELT (An Ancient Grain)

Spelt is an "Old World" grain that was used during the Roman period. It's basically an ancestor of wheat, but it has a lower gluten content than many modern-day wheat's and when milled is lighter than traditional whole meal flours.

White spelt flour is even lighter, and while it gives a cake-textured bread loaf on its own, the flavor is a delicious nutty taste, and the texture can be improved by mixing it with strong white bread flour.

It has a high protein content of 13%, but, like whole meal flour – does not translate to gluten forming potential. Spelt is often confused with another grain called "Emmes"-which is known as Farro in Italy. To add to the confusion, large grains of spelt may also be called "Farro Grande".

Spelt may be safely consumed by some people's wheat sensitivities, or those with certain intolerances, but unfortunately, not those afflicted with celiac disease.

Many bakers provide customers with this bread on a particular day's bake of the week, as a special incentive to those not knowingly sure of its properties. Many are smitten by its unique distinct nutty mellow flavor and texture and become hooked with its purchase. Spelt allows itself to marry well with other flours, such as oat flour, amaranth and wheat flour.

Spelt and blueberry scones make a delicious change from a fruited wheat scone.

Spelt Bloomer

450g Spelt flour	**RDT-26C.**	**Bake 200c. Time -35 mins.**
275g Water (37C.)	**BFT-90mins**	
30g Honey	**KB-45mins**	
7.5 Salt		
15g Fresh Yeast		
30g Oil		

White Spelt and Caraway Bread

Sponge	100g Water-24C.	Allow to stand for 2-3 hours at room temperature. **BFT 1-2 hours. Final proof -1-2 hours Tins sprayed, sprinkled with maize.**
	2g Fresh Yeast	
	100g White spelt flour.	
Dough	200g Water-24C.	
	7.5g Fresh Yeast	
	360g White spelt flour	
	7.5g Fine sea salt	
	25g Caraway seeds	

15. Community

What are bakeries – but basically a communal central hub,
Bringing people together – like it's some sort of social club,
Their relevance as important as any post office or food depot,
Butchers, fishmongers, coffee shops – cappuccino / espresso,
They allow for people to chat, purchase, congregate, smile,
They allow for small talk, long talk, work, art, music, lifestyle,
Its common knowledge that peoples love to confide and express,
Especially in an environment which can assist in detoxing stress,
The bakeries aroma acting as the lost leader-drawing people in,
Irrelevant of purchase or repose – just acknowledgement within,
That's the importance of the humble bakery keeping itself afloat,
Not just supplying breads, cakes with daily specials to promote,
The bakery also acts as a drop-in centre – a source of engagement,
Allowing people to feel they belong, reside without arrangement,
Uniting individuals to bond and coincide with others of the day,
Building the community which strengthens due to a baker's display,
You'll never find that in an instore Supermarket Bakery chain,
Where lifeless, soulless products, just appear and lie there in vain,
Nobody to talk to, no one's listening, like shopping in a morgue,
Disengagement – the order of the day-irrelevant of cobs or Coburg,
Community is central to our well-being, our sanity, mental health,
And Bakeries are at the forefront – not simply prospering for wealth,
Because without community, without that underlying co-operative,
Then bakeries will cease to be – exempt – not part of our prerogative.

16. Sandwiches

What is a Sandwich without the bread, is the Question?
But then what is Bread, without the role of the Baker,
Try a Bruschetta without it, or Burgers without the Bun,
A Cheese and ham Toastie, will need bread to succumb,
Pastrami without the Rye, or Salmon without the Bagel,
Fillings would not hold, and they would be unstable,
Wraps would not exist, they'd be no Bacon and Egg rolls,
Toasted Panini would disappear, like a magical Houdini.

French baguettes not around – that would be a crime,
Jaffles and Croque Monsieur, not as tasty or sublime,
Crispy Pork, pate, and Mayo missing its Bahn – Mi Rolls,
Foccacia Sandwiches a pipe dream-just Porchetta folds,
Try eating it without the bread, there's nothing to behold.
The Earl of Sandwich wouldn't approve, a history foretold,
Sandwiched croissant, steak sandwich, no hot dog rolls,
Sandwiches wouldn't exist, if not for Baker's heart and souls.

And what about that Borek, with its spicy lamb and cheese,
Difficult to consume without a blanket of dough to appease,
Chicken pesto, crying out for its Rosetta focaccia Italian roll,
Tuna salad without sourdough, now consumed from a bowl,
Spanish tomatoed Bocadillos, without its bread parcel to fill,
Eat in or take away, it doesn't matter, be it Madrid or Seville,
Sliders without brioche, pizza without base, no cheese Baps,
Sandwiches wouldn't exist; it would be turmoil and mishaps.

The fillings will take precedence, and are always highlighted,
Whether open, rolled or stacked, to keep customers excited,
And Bread being the carrier, becomes a secondary thought,
But what off the outcome, preparing one without the ought,
The sandwiches importance bears bonding the two together,
Because a sandwich is a marriage, not one without the other,
It's inequitably important that the two can merge and unite,
Making a sandwich something to behold, and bakers forthright.

17. 1758

Supposably an important date from a bread perspective, as it was in 1758 that the Earl of Sandwich so decided to place a slice of meat between two pieces of bread, and hence the so-called Sandwich as we know it today, became born, and eventually initiated.

Whether factually all is correct remains with historians to decide. As for Bakers, their journey began into what can only be described as a food revolution. Sandwiches slowly became part of the everyday diet, whether as a meal, snack, or a convenience product.

To put everything into perspective, the sandwich industry today accounts for a multi-billion-dollar industry globally, and accounts for staggering financial growth. The sandwich market size was valued at USD 11.27 billion in 2019, grew to 11.92 billion in 2023 and is poised to reach USD 18.46 Billion by 2031. The ever-increasing demand for ready-to-eat products is what drives the market growth, whether its breakfast sandwiches, traditional deli or café sandwiches, retail stores, restaurants, supermarkets, convenience stores, travel hubs, petrol stations, and related channels.

Sandwiches are part of life as we now know it, and acceptance of this trend is set to continue.

Sandwiches are comprised of some form of bread in whatever disguise. Bread is the foundation stone of the sandwich, and so therefore it is only correct to acknowledge the Bakers role in this configuration of financial disparity. If the sandwich market is to grow, then therefore the Baker and the Baking industry has a right to profit from this growth. It must be a shared evaluation, a compromise of not one gaining without the other. Sandwich makers in general will have never seen the inside of a bakery – and never will. They take a commercially made bread product, add fillings and garnishes, fancy labelling, packaging and put an increased profit margin on, one for their efforts and two for the sake of business acumen.

They may toast the sandwich, dress the sandwich, plate the sandwich, but at the end of the day, it's still a sandwich – which is comprised of bread. Many will argue that flour and water cost nothing, bread is tax free, and it's all cheap to produce. They won't account for the fact that bakers rise early, or work unsociable hours, get little acknowledgment or consideration for their task and physical labour. Automation plays its role in manufacture of bread, but it still must be controlled, maintained, organised and fed. A simple Bagel can be produced at a cost price of less than one dollar, yet with a filling can be sold for 9-15 dollars depending on the establishment and location. The markup is considerable, and this accounts for not only bagels, but for all varieties of breads, whether artisanal or simply retail/commercial operations.

Bakers must learn to join this growing trend – how to jump onto the bandwagon and not just concentrate on Baked loaves or sliced breads. They need to be players amongst fellow competitors to redress the balance of profiteering. It's their right as bakers to apply this crossroads, just as much as having a barista providing morning coffee to supplement sales of morning goods and sandwiches.

Sandwiches have reached a peak within the world of food consumption, and if the Earl of Sandwich was around today – would surely agree in redressing the balance.

18. The Power of Pastry

Pastry has the power to encapsulate,
It has direct symmetry.
It has an obscure movement.
It has the magic to allure.

The stance to bewitch.
The beauty to enthrall.
The taste to succumb too.
It has the strength to construct
Yet the fragility to crumble.

Pastry has the finesse to enrich.
It has glamour to grace.
It has the desirability to dazzle.
And the evocativeness to tantalise.

It has the richness to bequeath.

It has the splendor to speak.

It has the science to unravel.

It has the chemistry to unearth.

It has the pleasure to promote.

It has the opulence to enthrall.

The sweetness to seduce.

And the colour to mesmerise.

Pastry has the power -It's in your hands,

for you to withhold,

Its aesthetics, history, acknowledgment,

and credibility left for you to unfold.

19. The Wonder of Plunder

Danish Pastry – a laminated sweet dough as its commonly known,
Is also "Plunder" in Germanic, as acquired from the Austrian Zone,
Where Viennese Bakers laminated dough, using butter with turns,
And created sweet dough pastry, a product for which everyone yearns.

Plunder is a wonder – if you consider its versatility, uses, finishing,
Because this paste can be shaped in various forms, after pinning,
It can be rolled, twisted, folded, coiled, shaped, pressed or pleated,
And added to that, it can be baked or fried – offered cold or heated.

From one square, fifteen plus shapes can be made with this paste,
With a combination of fillings and fruits to please everyone's taste,
And if you include all the twists, knots, folds, and other shapes too,
You'll see why the wonder of plunder is a Bakers dream come true.

The resourcefulness of this paste has made it a pastry rubric cube,
A never-ending conundrum of ideas, even if twisted round a tube,
This pastry gave confectionery that added boost, a feeling of pride,
Even though today, a majority adopts croissant paste to preside.

Croissant pastes and plunder – are two different doughs,
Although considered to be the same, plunder is richer to compose,
Added sugar, fat, eggs, milk – it's much leaner and more forgiving,
And it provides a softer, tastier, easier eating item, plus garnishing.

Glazed as a painter demands, primed with egg wash after its rising,
Baked, an undercoating of apricot, a gloss of flavoured water icing,
This can then have additional garnishing, nuts, chocolate, and fruits,
A most acknowledged morning good, which "Plunder" contributes.

20. The Bakers Shift

You've got your coffee, and the radios turned on,
Its early morning starts, the day has just begun,
Dark outside, without a single person insight,
A solitary existence but for stars and moonlight.

Only the oven alarm to re-awaken the dream,
An office job, a 9-5, or life that could have been,
As Winter, Spring, Summer and Autumn rotate,
Loaves need to be baked and ordering to collate.

Paying bills, paying staff, paying the suppliers too,
Maintaining presence, ethics, through and through,
Hygiene the order of the day, precedence to be set,
Part of the picture, mindset, besides the profit net.

Customers need a smile, plus their daily loaves,
Proficient bakes, weighted, placed in neat rows,
The windows need polishing, lighting controlled,
The sparkle of energy, cleanliness left to unfold.

Packaging and drinks are another task included,
All part of the service, which can't be excluded,
Monitoring the time, temperature, air flow too,
The Bakers shift waits for whatever's next on que.

21. The Old Baker

The Old Baker looked white and pasty, lacking daylight, sunshine, and fresh air,

But when it came to knocking out cakes, he did it with gusto, panache, and flair,

The old Baker didn't have an Instagram account, in fact social media wasn't his life,

But this old boy had every recipe there was, stored in his head like honey in a hive,

The old Baker had stood the test of time, and overshadowed his fellow brothers,

With stamina, resilience, fortitude, but giving time, care, and assistance to others.

The old baker had a story to tell, happy to share his knowledge, wisdom, and skills,

No cotton-wool-filled stories, no nonsense, fluff, yarns, and no sugar-coated frills,

The old baker spoke as if it was, direct, truthful, to the point, just its black or white,

Honesty, integrity, transparency, how baking should be, when working day /night.

The old baker wasn't as fast as younger years, but was a trooper of our times,

Needed glasses to facilitate reading, but not for piping straight Viennese lines,

He had no trouble in moulding, knocking back, or energy /strength in kneading,

It was just the thermostat/ timer adjustments – required for the correct reading,

He couldn't stretch out as easily to reach the products and tools on the shelves,

But it was a dab hand at finishing products, professionally applying glazes and gels,

The old baker couldn't fit in for more than six hours a day, as it came to be as now,

As fatigue and tiredness were looming after the years, forged on hands and brow,

Bending the knees was a quest that was seldom applied when the job demanded,

But this old Baker was the King of cakes, whenever the request was commanded.

The old Baker was acquiring arthritis / rheumatism, repetitive strain injury too,

But it didn't stop him hand depositing muffins, cupcakes, and whatever taboo,

He didn't need convalescing, assistance, nurturing, and occasional hand helping,

Because the old baker could forge ahead, devoid of the elements surrounding,

Life had taught this old baker that resilience, reliability, were hallmarks required,

That self-control, self-belief, good ethics, a kind heart, and a listening ear attired,

Being good at your job was an asset, a tribute, a recommendation of pride,

That wisdom is acquired with age, irrespective of knowledge, experience aside,

And that to be recognised or leave what is known as a legacy of himself,

That humanity had to amplify more than just baking, -his lesson to ourselves.

22. Hybrid doughs

Sourdough bread is bread produced naturally,
But against the elements, it can at times act behaviorally,
The weather, the quality of flour, daily temperature too,
Can all affect the dough, and this is just to mention a few.

Sourdough not proving, rising, or simply not pushing,
Can give Baker's headaches, despair, expectations crushing,
Because it's impossible to sell, if it doesn't resemble bread,
A heavy lump of dough that feels, weighs, like a lump of lead.

It was for this reason that Bakers introduced the hybrid loaf,
Which marries culture and yeast, and a fermentation by both,
It simply is a safeguard, a safety net, call it whatever you will,
But it allowed the Bakers to reprieve, except for the anxiety pill.

Purists would scream, if knowing sourdough contained yeast,
And those with allergies and intolerances boycott you at least,
Many would frown and call it a crime of what bread resembles,
Others shame you on social media, or other active tech temples.

The fact remains that its widespread practice, and is nothing new,
Whether its Croissant, Danish, Donut or Scones requiring it too,
Hybrid doughs have been around since baking began,
And like press burger dough, it's a combination, a counter plan.

Press burger can be made separately or combine a mix of two,
A yeasted dough with shortbread pastes, blended as on queue,
Equal quantities of both resemble a paste base for wet fruits,
A hybrid dough of significance, renowned with Germanic roots.

A lump of fresh yeast thrown into a scone dough, unknowingly,
The addition of culture to whatever yeasted doughs – willingly,
Will make the product bloom and rise with better fermentation,
In the end, Hybrid doughs will prove themselves in presentation.

Hybrid doughs are not an excuse, and neither are they the answer,
But Baking, like other industries, sees binding acts as the enhancer,
Whether its cars, plants, animals, breeds, genetics, music collusion,
Or simply milk bread with classic Tangzhong and Brioche fusion.

Hybrid -a word not commonly associated with baking or produce,
But its relevant in many items, as with chefs cooking with verjuice,
Hybrid is common with baked goods, from cakes, cookies, desserts,
And hybrid is converting baking, with a reminder from past experts.

23. Bakers Prep List

Donuts, cruffins, cupcakes, pie,
Buns, scones, and loaves of rye,
Quiche, pastie, flans and tarts,
Cakes, Tortes, shortbread hearts.

Danish, croissant and cream horn,
Puff paste, Strudel of poppy mohn,
Slices, Brownie, Blondie and Bars,
Sponges, Chiffon, Cookies in Jars.

Buns, Bagels, Sticks and Knots,
Baguettes, Baps, floured high tops
Turkish, Ciabatta, Cobs and Splits,
Rolls dispersed using Bakers Mitts.

Fruitcakes, Mud cakes, Swiss rolls,
Vanilla slice pastes of multiple folds,
Fondant fancies, lemon meringue,
Fresh fruit tarts with a citrus tang.

Sausage rolls, pizza, scrolls, eclairs,
Buttercream cake of different layers,
Gingerbread, Icings and Traybakes,
Wedding, Novelty, Birthday cakes.

Ganache, marshmallow, Gluten free,
Baked meringues with colour spree,
Turnovers, rock cakes, coconut macs,
Flourless cakes in the bakers' racks.

The list is daunting, the day is short,
So, strategy – logistics are at thought,
Using the concept of winning the day,
The Bakers mind puts defeatism away.

It's tough, it's a push, it's another day,
So, nothing changes from our role play,
The concept of pleasing hungry masses,
Our duty bound divert of social classes.

24. Dough Recipe

Sourdoughs

White

Ingredient	%	4Kg	5Kg	6Kg
White flour	90	3.600	4.500	5.400
Semolina	10	0.400	0.500	0.600
Salt	2.5	0.100	0.125	0.150
Gluten	1	0.040	0.050	0.060
Culture	35	1.400	1.750	2.100
Water	48	1.920	2.400	2.880
Olive oil	1	0.040	0.050	0.060

Rye

Ingredient	%	2Kg	3Kg	5Kg
White flour	35	0.700	1.050	1.750
Rye Meal	65	1.300	1.950	3.250
Salt	2.5	0.050	0.075	0.125
Gluten	8.5	0.170	0.255	0.425
Culture	35	0.700	1.050	1.750
Water	71	1.420	2.130	3.550
Olive oil	2	0.040	0.060	0.100

Grain

Ingredient	%	7kg	9Kg	11kg
Grain mix	35	2.450	3.150	3.850
Water	59.5	4.165	5.355	6.545
Bakers flour	65	4.550	5.850	7.150
Salt	2.5	0.175	0.225	0.275
Gluten	5	0.350	0.450	0.550
Culture	35	2.450	3.150	3.850
Olive oil	1.5	0.105	0.135	0.165

Wholemeal

Ingredient	%	2Kg	3Kg	5Kg
Wholemeal	100	2.000	3.000	5.000
Salt	2.5	0.050	0.075	0.125
Gluten	5	0.100	0.150	0.250
Culture	35	0.700	1.050	1.750
Water	61	1.220	1.830	3.050
Olive Oil	1	0.020	0.030	0.050

Soft Doughs

Ingredient	%	9Kg	14Kg	16Kg
White				
Bakers flour	100	9000	14000	16000
Salt	2	0.180	0.280	0.320
Improver	1	0.090	0.140	0.160
Yeast	0.6667	0.060	0.093	0.107
Water	60	5.400	8.400	9.600
Veg Oil	1	0.90	0.140	0.160

Ciabatta

Poolish	%	3Kg	4kg	5Kg
Bakers flour	1.56	2.08	2.6	
Water	1.56	2.08	2.6	
Yeast	0.002	0.003	0.004	
Bakers flour	100	3000	4000	5000
Salt	3	90	120	150
Yeast	0.7	0.021	0.028	0.035
Water	18	0.540	0.720	0.900
Olive oil	4.6	0.138	0.184	0.230

Grain

Ingredient				
Grain	%	9Kg	14Kg	16 Kg
Grain mix	30	2.700	4.200	4.800
Water	63	5.670	8.820	10.080
Bakers flour	70	6.300	9.800	11.200
Salt	2	0.180	0.280	0.320
Improver	1	0.090	0.140	0.160
Gluten	5	0.450	0.700	0.800
Yeast	0.6667	0.060	0.093	0.107
Veg Oil	1	0.090	0.140	0.160

Sweet

Ingredient	%	3KG	3.5k	4kG
Bakers flour	100	3000	3.500	4.000
Salt	1.5	0.045	0.053	0.063
Improver	1.5	0.045	0.053	0.060
Sugar	10	0.300	0.350	0.400
Yeast	1.134	0.040	0.047	0.053
Egg	100	3000	3.500	4.000
Cream	10	0.300	0.350	0.400
Water	40	1.200	1.400	1.600
Butter	3	0.090	0.105	0.120

25. X, ant

X, ant – is French abbreviation for croissant, easily inscribed,
And as with croissants, there's no faith or disciplines to hide,
But somehow, somewhere, they've rearisen as a new shrine,
Over sophistication, entering the realms of rare vintage wine.

How has this simple laminated crescent shaped piece of dough,
Elevated itself to become more than most baked goods bestow,
Is there such a thing as croissant academy, or a croissant science,
Or is it simply a set off rules, with a form of followed compliance.

Because croissants are produced in a multitude of many ways,
And each has its own entity and production in whichever phase,
Doughs are made either straight, or using a sponge or ferment,
Others rested overnight in the fridge, lamination the final stent.

The fats can differ in various ways, but Butter is recommended,
Either purchased pads to simplify the task, unsalted represented,
Cultured butters are all the new trend, but costs can be incurred,
Others use cooking butter blended with flour, if that is preferred.

The croissant shapes can be cut out using a pastry croissant roller,
Others prefer to measure precisely, with a knife and a metal ruler,
Some use automated rollers, which can cut, roll, shape all in one,
And weights vary from 90 to 120 grams, pending on cost overrun.

Some are rolled straight, others traditionally in a crescent form,
Colours can be included, striped, two tone, or plain to conform,
Fillings are another option, added before the croissant is rolled,
Varying from savoury to sweet, with an added topping when sold.

Egg washed before baked, either with brush or electric spray gun,
They can be left plain on removal of the oven, or syruped as a bun,
Flavoured honey can be warmed and brushed on the surface area,
And garnishes can be sprinkled, to add a finished style "contraria".

All in all, the world of the croissant has become an entity of its own,
From Nutella, pistachio and chocolate, it proves how they've grown,
The almond, caramel, biscoff, plus the fresh strawberry and cream,
Has made the quest of the croissant, the baker / pastrycooks dream.

Some Croissant differentials (to list a few – but the door is open to creative input)
- Sourdough croissant,
- Danish paste croissant
- Charcoal croissant
- Matcha croissant
- Puff pastry croissant

- Chocolate croissant
- Apple crumble croissant
- Savoury Ham and Cheese (unglazed)
- Savoury Cheese and Tomato (unglazed)

26. Celebrity Bakers

Celebrity bakers are a breed, that's very few and far between,
In fact, it's possible to ascertain that they're practically unseen,
We seem confounded and saturated with "The Celebrity chef",
But when it comes to Bakers, eyes closed – ears seemingly deaf.

The question at hand, is why this has arisen, and if so, the case,
When baking requires stamina, fortitude at equally intense pace,
The uniform differs slightly, the product a different connotation,
But just as important profession, without unethical denunciation.

To re-affirm, there are several Bakers whose names could apply,
But in general, they're the 1%, and not the remaining other guy,
Put into perspective, they're groomed by the media to perform,
From this stardom arises, like doughs shaped/ moulded to form.

The fact to engage with, is that everyone and anyone can bake.
As baking is a domestic entity, a hobby, a therapy, my cupcake,
It's a language, a friend, a gift, and whatever the need perceived,
Home baking with mother and children, fun to fulfill their need.

Trying to find the illusive Celebrity Baker is possibly a task in itself,
The who's who of the baking books, now for sale on the bookshelf,
Names and personas that you've never heard off and seen before,
Begging the question, to when and where is the "Maestro's Encore"

The Maestro, Celebrity Baker, Aficionado, call them what you wish,
Those that convey knowledge, wisdom, experience to any given dish,
Seldom seen, seldom heard and hidden from everyday deliberations,
Overshadowed by their cooking counterparts without appreciations.

But don't lose sight or lose faith, the 1% is here performing on que,
And remember to acknowledge them, amongst the beleaguered few,
For they are upholding the status of the profession, as a shining light,
Allowing others to continue, with what matters and the added insight.

27. The Bakers Creed

My culture, my starter, my feed,
My mother, my ferment, my deed,
I'll nurture it, care for it, honour it,
Love it, befriend it, bequeath it.

Flour and water simply blended,
Temperature and time co-friended,
The addition of Rye or wheatgerm,
Allowing for growth so to reaffirm.

Coaxed, cared for, gently applied,
Proving indispensable as required,
Kept at ambient room temperature,
Or in the cold room, slowly to mature.

This driving force, this central core,
An essential addition of yeast spore,
Also known and referred to as sour,
Giving doughs credibility on the hour.

Its old, its new, it's an inoculation,
Important in baking of any nation,
A simple antidote that's undermined,
Adding it allows quality to be defined.

If you protect and maintain its keep,
It will aid you to gather and to reap,
It will provide protection and uphold,
Products baked, purchased and sold.

28. Yeast

What is yeast – but just a simple living micro – organism,
A bacterium, culture, natural fungi, a fermentable prism,
Yeast simply comes from the air that is full of wild spores,
Lying around us on leaves, tree bark, skins of fruits pores.

These yeasts are carried by soil, dust, insects and birds,
And accumulate with moisture, warmth, and food incurs,
They'll only multiply if under these conditions and terms,
And remain a mystery and magical, natures hidden germs.

In ancient times wine making and brewing were entwined,
Produced in the same proximity with the bakery combined,
It was the fermenting liquor spilling into the baking trough,
Thus, allowing leavened breads to rise, provide the payoff.

A formation of grain and yeast, time and fermenting liquor,
Created the barm, so as to produce doughs proved in wicker,
The barm – it's a word not commonly used in today's society,
Yet in days gone by, its how bakers made their loaves reliably.

The barm -yeast, was produced in various ways and methods,
A mash of grain, malted barley, rye, flour or boiled potatoes,
Anything which would produce a reliable, stable fermentation,
Convert to sugar and then alcohol, a recipe of yeast activation.

There exist many recipes for barms, from the years gone by,
But raw materials and taxes, made home brewing costs high,
As ale and beers were the source material to create the barm,
Without alcohol to ferment, the process would have to disarm.

Many professional Bakers continued to use the method Barm,
Even when compressed yeast was available, it couldn't charm,
Because they believed it provided more flavour, better bread,
And they built a high reputation, using their own yeast instead.

But eventually convenience soon became the order of the day,
Using the compressed yeast cake, easy to access and to weigh,
It changed completely how Bakeries worked, processed bread,
Quick, efficient, reliable, for bakers it became their homestead.

From this came the introduction of dried yeast in granular form,
Twice as potent as compressed yeast when in water lukewarm,
A little added sugar, a time schedule, and it will grow activated,
A product with a shelf life, no fridge required, baking updated.

Finally, we have instant yeast, easy to incorporate, and ambient,
Guaranteed success without fermentation and totally compliant,
It's become the answer to Baking where facilitation is required,
Or used as a safety net when Fresh yeast ages, or turns expired.

29. Plaited Bread

What's the purpose of plaited bread?
When dough placed in tins -is far easier instead,
Why spend time making numerous strands of dough?
Only to be confused as to contemplate where they go.

If you look around there are many forms of braiding,
From simple single strand knots to 12 strands in the making.
But the issue is not the actual number of strands of dough,
More so the reasoning – why do Bakers perform this show?

Braiding is steeped in history, dating back 30,000 years,
And started with hair, a contribution derived from our peers,
Later came fabrics and rugs and all manner of intricate weaving,
Adopted by Bakers to give the Profession kudos and meaning.

The origins of braided bread date back to the 15th Century,
With a famous Swiss bread, named "Zopf," and woven coincidentally,
To represent a braid of hair, a practice still enacted by Bakers today,
Be it 3, 4 or 6 strands or more, resembling arms intertwined on display.

Plaited Bread

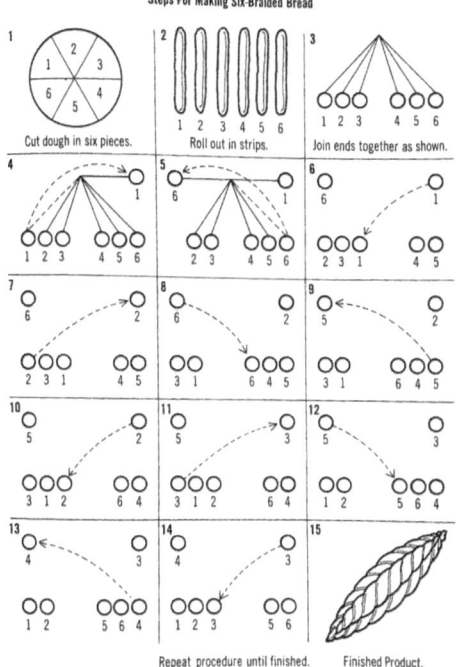

Steps For Making Six-Braided Bread

History depicts in ancient times that when a married man died,
For his wife to follow him to the grave and be buried by his side,
But in later times, the deceased wife was replaced by a braid of her hair,
Which through time evolved, becoming a loaf of bread as a compare.

The essence of the braid is simple – it's to represent and symbolise love,
Three strands of braided breads symbolise truth, justice, peace, -thereof,
While 12 strands of bread denote the miracle of the 12 loaves of bread,
By which a double decked braid can be stacked, using 2 loaves instead.

Most Braids are kept straight, others woven round or heart shaped,
And each country has their own version and style, glazed, and baked,
Braided bread exists in every European culture with differing names,
Be it Challah, Houska, Chalka, Tsoureki – all born from various grains.

There's Brioche, Bosman, Hefezopf, Vanocka, Kulich, to add to the list,
All braided, woven, plaited and then glazed and garnished as a co-exist,
They're all identified by their makers and finished with tradition comply,
An expectation at Festive events, weddings, and if religion does apply.

Braiding today can teach us many things, hands, and mind combined.
It forces you to be patient, focused and requires physicality aligned,
Fluidity of movement is necessary, addressing feet, shoulders, arms lose,
Thus, allowing the hands to perform, gently, patiently, without excuse.

30. Weights in Bakery

Weights and measures apply to all retail and wholesale transactions where measurement determines price.

Consistency and certainty in measurement supports fair and open competition and it makes all businesses, regardless of their size or financial strength, follow the same rules.

Bread and Bakery goods items are either sold by number or weight. The National Measurement Act of 1960 and the National Trade Measurement Regulations 2009 – regulate how bread and bakery goods /products are sold by measurement.

The NMI employs trade inspectors throughout the country. They ensure that sellers are following the correct process. If an inspector finds that you are short-measuring your customers – you could be fined up to 200,000 Australian dollars which converts to approximately 100,000 pounds sterling.

Items sold by weight include biscuits, and cookies in packs of more than one and pre-packaged bread.

In smaller establishments – you are not required to sell non packaged loaves of bread by weight.

A servicing license verifies the scales after each repair or adjustment. Responsibility is placed on the ownness of the company to make sure the scale is correct at all time.

Using Scales

If using a scale to weigh and sell bread and bakery items that aren't pre-packaged – you must ensure the following,

1. The National Measurement Institute (NMI) has approved your type of scale and any attached modules.

2. A service license has verified your scales and attached modules.

3. You and your staff use the scales in the correct manner (levelling and indicating zero /tare before use)

4. You position your retail scales in a position where the customer can easily see any weighing process.

5. The Bakery scales should be in a fixed stable position -and moved only as a necessity.

31. Kilo-Weight

Primarily, weights in Bakeries were in Imperial measurement – Pounds and Ounces.

This was before the introduction of metric conversion, which took place to Kilo and grams in Australia in July 1974. In the UK it changed in 1965, which interestingly was eight years before it joined the European Union.

Cup measurement – both still popular and customary in Australia and the USA – are more often used in domestic and home baking – and while they are reliable and quick – they don't account this method of measuring as an accurate form of weight.

Weighing equates to accuracy.

Even liquids in Bakery are advised to be weighed as opposed to measured – unless programmed through a water /temperature quantity control meter.

Balance scales are similarly out and have been replaced with metric digital scales and spring scales are seldomly ever used in professional establishments.

Because items must be weighed and programmed to follow set formulas and recipes, it's essential that scales become a major player within a bakery. They must be respected, cleaned, charged, maintained, and regularly calibrated.

Guess work will accommodate certain properties and goods – but the bottom line and crunch of the motto is that weighing accounts for standardization. This then leads to consistency, and this is then followed through with guarantees.

All in All – it's a simple equation – one which can't be juggled with or overlooked. Although "Kilo" is a four-letter word – it's a friendly one – a useful one. A little like "Tare" on the scales these words resonate with bakery as does time with a clock.

The Kilo was introduced from France as a more accurate method of weight and dispersion-and it proved to be much more accurate than the imperial weights and measures. The fact you can account for one gram in weight on the scales indicates its relevance and importance.

The relevance of the Kilo can't be underestimated. Inspired by the French revolution, scientists at the time wanted to start fresh on a new consistent system of measurement, basing units not on arbitrary mandates from past Kings – but on Nature. The goal was to create a system of measurement "for all time -for all people." When the international Bureau of Weights and Measures was founded in France in the late 1800s the meter – the standard unit of length – was created to be one ten-millionth of the distance from the North Pole to the equator. The gram takes inspiration from the density of water – it's equal to the mass of one cubic centimeter of water held at 4-degree C.

To disseminate these new units – to make sure that everyone in the World understood them – the inventors of the metric system decide to create physical objects to embody and define them.

They crafted a metal bar to be exactly 1 Meter long.

They created Big K to represent the mass of 1 Kilogram or 1000 grams.

Since the 19TH Century, all physical relics of the old metric system have been replaced by measurements affixed to constant forces of nature. The meter was originally defined as a proportion of the size of the Earth. But even the shape of the world isn't permanent.

So today the meter is defined by the speed of light, The second is affixed to the motion of the atoms of the element cesium.

Only the Kilograms is still defined by a physical object.

Although new ongoing science in France is still trying to define the Kilo, using what is known as a Kibble balance – named after the late inventor British physicist Bryan Kibble – sometimes referred to as a Watt balance – to redefine the Kilo – it uses mass, velocity, gravitational pull, magnetism and electricity do define a constant.

What is the reason for this?

Supposably more accurate control will replace the big K in France because it will know the mass of a Kilo in terms of a constant. And that will provide a precise measurement, a way to keep ensuring a Kilo remains a Kilogram, that can be used to weigh objects and determine their mass according to the new standard. Now – quality assurance on the Big K is based on agreement.

Quality assurance on the Kibble balance is that it's based on a constant of nature that has been measured rigorously by the entire World.

The bottom line of the above information is this,

In the future we will no longer need a government or an International governing body to tell us what a Kilogram is. It will be a fundamental truth of the Universe, available to anyone with the proper equipment to realise it. The kibble balance will allow for absolute measurement and in the future the manufacturing industry won't need to send their weights and scales for calibration – they will have a Kibble balance on their factory floor.

In that light, the new definition is more democratic – one that is free to be used throughout the World.

Philosophically it means – that the Kilogram will soon be defined by the fundamentals of the Universe, not some human machination.

In the meantime – the Kilo remains the Kilo. The most precise, accurate and user-friendly mode of weighing used by Bakers.

32. Sourdough

Sourdough – it's become the "in" word with bread today,
Though its existence stems beyond the pyramids -fermented by sunray,
Promoted, embossed, and printed on every café menu,
Conducive to health, well-being and baked daily just for you.

Inexpensive to produce but expensive to purchase,
It's all about colour, crust and that chewy interior,
Upping the "Artisan "quirk, while aiming to be bespoke and upmarket,
More style over substance propaganda – with sales the ongoing target.

And it's in vogue, on the TV, within the media and the talk of the town,
During lockdown and isolation, its everyone's go to the therapist,
Creating one's own starter and nurturing it like a pet,
What other product exists, bonding as friend, companion, life source and interconnect.

Wholesome, natural fermentation, bread as it traditionally should be,
Uncontaminated, no chemical additives, rustic, earthy, simplistic unanimous plea,
Stamped with the "Real Bread" signatures campaign for authenticity,
Digestive aid, improved flavour, longer shelf life – recommended for all to see.

Bread as it always was – just tweeted, reincarnated, the awaited renaissance,

Nothing new, nothing invented, nothing unique – just a return to time and patience,

All the noise, media rants and nutritional and food allergy therapists decree,

When it's simply a U-turn, back to basics, reality and advocating the word "Purity."

33. Lamination

Lamination of doughs and pastes is both a skill and an art,
Building multiple layers, whilst keeping two elements apart,
It's a process which requires time and both attention to detail,
Creating layers with intricate folds, providing results not to fail.

Texture and temperature will equate to a given outcome,
Dough and fat being cold is the general rule of thumb,
Plasticised, malleable, conditioned, texturised fat is necessary,
The dough has the same texture, and free from excess flour dust.

For puff pastry and vienoisserie pastes to rise,
Requires a form of levitation that assists in increasing their size,
And although yeast action will aerate and rise a given dough
Added lamination enables the lift, flakiness, and ability to grow.

Now lamination isn't a task you should perform by hand,
Its better if you engage with a Pastry sheeter – electrically manned,
Another factor is to prepare laminated doughs earlier in the day,
Because at noon the temperature rises, and fats moisten like soft clay.

Cultured dry Butter or fabricated laminating fats are a perfect addition,
To facilitate the creating of layers and turns with this ongoing mission,
Because once completed -solidified in the fridge – ready for process,
it will be noted the layers will have amounted into a formidable excess.

Lamination will give strength, structure, stability, insulation appearance,
It will provide taste, texture, lift and offer guaranteed assurance,
It allows for products to become lighter, more digestible, and enjoyable,
And finally, it adds refinement and elegance, from a more employable paste.

Lamination allows a product to rise approximately five-seven-fold,
And can create layers counting over 800 for products to be sold,
It aerates Pie tops, sweet/ savoury Turnovers, Pasties and Sausage rolls,
In addition to adding flakiness to Croissants, Danish and Cinnamon scrolls.

Vanilla sliced pastry would remain dense, heavy, if it wasn't for lamination.
Rolled Cornettos would be bound in a tight coil -void of vivid expectation,
Cheese straws would remain simply cheese sticks, no light delicate finesse,
And without lamination, the use of pastes in bakery would simply digress.

34. Healthy Bread

What is it that constitutes the meaning healthy bread?
Is it the bran content or is it being gluten free instead?
Is it High protein and low carb or being premium quality,
Or baked fresh with time, care, and love as a commodity,
Should they be 5 seeded, 7 seeded, or 9 seeded loaves,
Whole grains, multi – grain, or sprouted grains suppose,
Is it the fact they should be thin sliced, rustic or artisan?
Or wood fired, bricked oven baked, or Dutch hot oven,
Should it be sourdough, fermented 12,18, or 36 hours,
Or malted granary, wheatgerm or made with rye sours,
Vegan is another option, no animal goods implemented,
No honey, egg, dairy fat or natural yoghurt represented,
Organic flours are another consideration to be included,
And whether the salt/sodium levels are to be excluded,
Does the bread contain any sugars, as a yeast food agent?
Or additives and preservatives as part of the engagement,
Many may argue that folic acids and minerals are a must,
Soluble fibre, vitamins and Iron content, a necessary just,
But are added hydrogenated fats and emulsifiers required,
While magnesium and potassium are befittingly attired,
Should milk be the healthiest option,

Or added oatmeal, quinoa, chia, barley as another addition,

How about Sorghum, Buckwheat, Millet, Spelt or Emmer,

Amaranth, Einkorn or Sonora flours added to the dilemma,

In the end what really matters, is how bread is conceived,

And that relates to personal taste and how its appeased,

Freshly baked bread is healthy bread, its man's staple food,

And as long as its enjoyed and tasty, it's hard to be improved.

35. Pies – Pyes

Pies – Savoury, sweet, Square, oval and round,
Baked, Steamed, Air Fried, with a history renowned,
They're integral to the Bakers/ Pastrycooks repertoire,
Whether produced in house or delivered from afar.

Imagine a Bakery without a selection of pies,
And then hear the public's outrage, fury, and cries,
Bakers have a responsibility to provide this humble delight,
It's a national treasure, made of butter or vegetable solite.

It's estimated each Australian eats 12 meat pies a year.
That's a total of 270 million per annum, with or without beer,
In New Zealand, the average is 15 meat pies - 66million a year,
And the UK – 1 billion pounds per annum of pies -a new frontier.

Pork pies contribute to huge sales – mince pies at Xmas too,
Shepherds /cottage pies, American/ Dutch apple pies, to name a few,
Pecan, Blueberry, Cherry – all affiliated to the global phenomenon,
As are fish, spinach, cheese and pumpkin, the list roles on and on.

Pies are historic, the earliest records date back to the 12th Century,
"Pyes" crust referred to as "Coffyn," with filing and paste rudimentary,
The pies were made of fowl, pigeon, eels, oysters, mussels, and rabbit,
But the first pies ever, were Egyptians who began this infamous habit.

History has shown us they encased honey filings with oats and wheat,
Before the Romans bought pies to Europe which included fish and meat,
The first published roman recipe is Rye crusted goat cheese and honey pie,
Documented in the Oxford English Dictionary, an early 14th Century testify.

Pies have been around forever and a day, its testimony to their popularity.
And they're not going anywhere, as time has proved from earnest familiarity,
They're as popular and continuously requested today as in times gone bye,
The redeeming quality of bakers/ pastrycooks – so pies can form our greatest ties.

36. Beer and Bread

Yeast concocted.

Fermentation necessary

Essential cultures used.

Harmful bacteria disposed of.

Both use similar processes.

Both acquiring flavour through time.

Without any yeast – it wouldn't exist

Thank nature and the earth's crust.

Man's staple food-beer align.

Barley, hops, yeast, and Adam's wine

A recipe that's lasted over the centuries

Proven as one of life's greatest discoveries.

And now it's a marriage, but it's not new,

Beer used in Bread, whatever the brew,

It aids fermentation, delivers that volume,

A bread with flavour, colour and bloom.

Beer and Bread were meant to be aligned.

Its nature's answer to life and mankind

Two essential commodities never relinquished.

Without it our loss, then forever impoverished

Beer and Bread

37. Pastry Work

(Patisserie –Konditorie –Pasticceria)

Pastry work is like Art – in the sense it contains no boundaries.

It allows itself to be stretched to limitless, unknown entities and covers every possible interpretation as to what is, what isn't, and what will be or what could be.

(When we think we know it all –we think again)

In pastry as in art, we find that what will please one, will not necessary please another. What infatuates some will disillusion others, what excites and stimulates can also dismiss and cause angst and bewilderment.

What gives – can also take, and what encompasses can also isolate.

Aesthetics can't be taught but can be controlled. A little like emotions and adrenalin, pastry must be controlled to some degree for it to be balanced correctly. The term "too flash in the pan", can be just as off putting, as too much "blandness and apathy".

Testosterone and femininity also need to be addressed in this multi – diverse industry. Striking the accepted balance is the order of the day, between gender differences, irrespective of equalities, creeds, and cultures.

Pastry doesn't discriminate, segregate, complicate!

But pastry must invigorate, encapsulate, intoxicate, infatuate and assimilate.

Pastry as in art has an important role to play. It must by its own standing, allow people to come together, allow them to bond, unify, and most importantly allow them to celebrate life.

Pastry is simply a catalyst – it's a merging of thoughts, ideas, concepts, tastes, and people.

Art is freedom – Pastry is Art!

38. Confected

The term confectionery can be translated into many forms, either that of Flour confectionery, sugar confectionery or chocolate confectionery.

Each branch has its own unique industry, with its own principles, skills, terminology, and products. They all lie under the same umbrella and are all related to some degree. For example, an iced chocolate donut requires yeast and fermentation knowledge, while the icing combines the art and skill of tempering soft fondant icing with the addition of prepared chocolate, be it in a liquid, paste, powdered or decorating form. Although this simple product may simplify the equation of all three entities, it by no means exemplifies the complexities and professional commitment required to expose confectionery daily.

The confectionery industry has a unique history dating back earlier than can be recorded. Grains have been crushed and moistened as a form of food since the beginning of time, sucking on sugar cane and honey as natural sweeteners provided energy and sustenance, and cocoa pods deemed not only as a food, and worshipped as a gift to mankind, even as currency, added mystique and health properties that scientists even today can't quite fathom. Relating these findings, it's possible to embellish the three practices and categorise them together in today's requirements. It's easy to forget that the three industries are Worlds apart, but are one common industry, all united in providing foodstuffs, pleasure, contentment and happiness.

No other industry has such a wealth of history, such a vast degree of complexities, and yet encapsulates such a credit to humans, helping to sustain daily requirements, fend off hunger and display products which bring colour, joy and instantaneous appeal to each one.

Confectionery somehow seems too feeble a word to comprehend its importance in society, easily surpassed in the modern world as just something sweet-full stop. But if you care to delve into its depths and hidden past, take the time to travel and view its vast entity, try to break into its closed cell doors, you will see that confectionery stems further and deeper than one book could ever justify.

It's worth enlightening the concepts within the confectionery world, be it flour, sugar or chocolate to form a guiding light along its enduring, forgiving, stimulating and hopefully, rewarding path.

39. Did you know (Pastry/Bakery Trivia)

1. Red velvet is a cocktail – (Cider, blackcurrant and Guinness)
2. Whisky brings out the flavour of strawberries.
3. The cocoa tree is bi-sexual.
4. Cocoa beans contain over 200 natural chemical components.
5. Orange Cointreau liqueur was created for women.
6. Clear copper pans / boilers, (unlined) help to retain the colour of fruit when cooking.
7. Michele Ferrero was the world's most successful confectioner, (Nutella)
8. The Black Sapote is also known as the chocolate fruit.
9. Only female bees sting when searching for pollen for honey
10. The king of fruits is the Durian, and the queen of fruits is the Mangosteen.
11. Coffee is a food, not a drink.
12. The Breadbasket of the world was in North Africa, during the Roman Empire (millions of acres of wheat)
13. Rice paper is not made from rice flour.
14. Coconuts are not nuts, they're "drupes" or commonly known as stone fruits.

15. A kiwi fruit supposably contains ten times more vitamin C, than an Orange.
16. The ethanol content in star anise fruit is 16 times sweeter than normal sucrose.
17. Milk powder added to a bagel mix will give a crispier shell and a mellow interior – but this can only be applied to non-kosher establishments, as milk and meat cannot be mixed under kosher ruling.
18. Fresh milk, buttermilk, and fresh ripened bananas are essential ingredients in Banana bread to acquire softer eating qualities.
19. Bananas are purchased in hands and mastic spice is graded in size by tears,
20. Pineapples once picked do not ripen, they only rot,
21. Making your own wedding cake is regarded as being superstitiously unlucky,
22. Walnuts can only be harvested once fallen from the tree,
23. Originally, cappuccino coffee was dusted with cinnamon, not chocolate,
24. Strawberries are the only fruit where the seeds grow on the outside of the fruit, approximately 200 per fruit.
25. Dried vine fruits are cut at the stem, then left on the vine to age and sweeten before being harvested.
26. Poppy seeds should be crushed – as opposed to ground when preparing a paste. Bitter to the taste as a seed, but sweeter on the tongue when crushed.

27. In earlier times, ornate chocolate boxes, once the contents consumed, were used as a lady's glove box.

28. Zakyntose in Greece, like Montelimart in France is famous for its nougat. Occupied up to 1936 by the Italian venetians, the island was never occupied by Turks, and the confection was an Italian tradition.

29. Rocky road was aptly named to face the great depression in America in 1929 after the stock market crash. Created by Joseph Edy and William Dryer, it was named to give people something to smile about during the depression.

30. The three C, s of baking, are Crust, Colour and Crumb.

31. Although the Quince fruit is normally associated with all things sweet, originally during early Roman / Greek times it was a substitute for potato and was served with roast goose, rosemary, and served with chestnuts and a sweet red wine sauce.

32. The champagne melon and the watermelon are both seeded from the same gene and are both from the same origins within South Africa.

33. Fernand Point, author of the cuisine bible "Ma Gastronomie", was responsible for creating the famous layered Marjolaine cake.

34. Classic Greek orange cake incorporates dried phyllo pastry mixed in to the batter, and thus absorbing the liquid of orange and syrup poured over once baked.

35. Watercress was commonly known and sold as poor man's bread in Victorian London.

36. Nuggets of Jaggery – (unrefined pure sugar) – are given to workers in India where there is lots of dust in the workplace – to help clear the lungs.

37. In Argentina when making fresh dulce de leche, glass marbles are used in the pan to replicate stirring or movement, this to prevent the milk from catching on the base of the pan and burning.

38. Your hands and fingers are the best thermometer in any kitchen.

39. Egg shells make for good compost on soil.

40. Romani – Gypsies often offered to re-tin /reline copper saucepans as part of their livelihood and travelling lives. Like travelling knife sharpeners.

41. Ciabatta bread wasn't introduced to the public until 1981. The Italians wanted a bread which could compete with the French baguette and so introduced this form of bread in slipper form, the most famous being the Panini roll which became the toasted sandwich to have.

42. The inventor of compressed yeast – died the second richest man in the world after Henry Ford at that time.

43. There are over 300 variants of wattle seed available in Australia.

44. Sticky toffee pudding was originally known as Sticky date pudding.

45. Bla –Bla –Bla, the Irish known Batch Bread, which was awarded GPI status in 2013 by the European Commission. This status protects all regional and local foods assuring their reputation as authentic.

46. Cocoa was first used and recognised as a Spice.

47. Hartshorn – was the name given to a product made up from ground up deer antlers – dating back to the Middle Ages – to make baking products light and fluffy – reacting like ammonia bicarbonate. (Hart – the British name for a male stag)
48. Figs are not a fruit, they are a syconium. (A tree stem that has expanded into a sac and contains flowers)
49. It requires 17,000 litres of water to produce One Kilo of Chocolate
50. Duck or Goose feathers were used primarily as pastry brushes in advent of bristle brushes – to apply egg washes and glazes.
51. Panko breadcrumbs are made from bread that's not baked – merely injected with an electrical current. They are used for coatings, pane and crumbing.
52. Margarine was created in France – renowned as a butter nation. It was invented in 1869 by the pharmacist "Mege – Mouries" at the request of Napoleon III to assist during the Franco-Prussian war. It's less expensive to produce than butter and keeps readily for longer periods.
53. The Macadamia nut is named after the Scottish Botanist – John Macadam. Aboriginal peoples originally called it 'Kindal-Kindal, Bauple, or Jindil.
54. The current record holder for the world's largest wedding cake is a 15,032 pounds made by Chefs at the Mohegan Sun Hotel and Casino in Connecticut and displayed at their New England Bridal showcase in 2004.

55. Fougasse – the French oil-based bread – which is meant to resemble a palm fond – was originally used by Bakers to check if the oven was at the right temperature for baking other breads.

56. In Egyptian days, it's noted that Bakers would have been stoned to death if their bread cultures had not worked or had been destroyed.

57. Emmer wheat is one of the first cereals domesticated in the old world dating back 3000 years. The romans called it "Pharaoh's wheat" because it was the most common type of wheat in ancient Egypt.

58. A bakery in Chester England, created the world's most expensive wedding cake valued at $52.7 Million – approximately – 28 million pounds sterling. It took more than 4000 diamonds to decorate the eight – tiered confection.

59. A good quality couverture chocolate should have 5-7 different flavours, and an exceptional couverture up to 12 differing flavour notes.

60. Products baked in the oven are deemed ready by their aroma – not by timers or constant opening of doors.

61. Spiced buns were banned in the UK when the English broke ties with the Catholic Church in the 16th Century. However, by 1592, Queen Elizabeth I relented and granted permission for commercial bakers to produce the buns for funerals, Christmas and Easter.

62. Horse Bread was the most common bread produced by Bakers in the early 1800,s and was a combination of oats, barley and any other grains and seeds, that could be incorporated into a dough. It was also a common bread eaten amongst the poor and destitute, during that period of hardship and poverty.

63. In Greece in early days, it was stated that to make a starter dough, you must use blessed water from the church with a basil leaf left inside, then add flour and allow to ferment slowly.

64. Modern methods to create a starter dough in Greece – use chickpeas in lukewarm water on top of the oven – and when there are signs of a white froth / slight fermentation on the surface, remove the chickpeas and use this water to create the starter dough with the addition of flour.

65. Tahini can be used to grease baking cake tins – tahini is pure sesame fat (100%) made from hulled and not unhulled sesame. This not only provides non-stick – it also provides additional flavour.

66. Until 1851, Corn-starch was used primarily for starching laundry. A method to produce pure culinary starch from Maize was patented by John Polson of Brown &Polson in Paisley, Scotland in 1854 and was sold as "Patented Corn Flour".

67. Two thirds of the world's consumption of breads – are Flat Breads.

68. Bakers Yeast and humans share 18% of their genes.

69. One jar of Nutella is sold somewhere in the World every 2.5 seconds

70. Black diamond apples and the white ghost apple supposably taste sweeter than honey. (A rare variety from the family of Huaniu apples that is cultivated from the Tibetan region of Nyingchi.)

71. Grissini – commonly known as Bread sticks were created to prevent the spread of disease. Antonio Brunero, a Baker from Turin was asked by the Duke Vittorio Amadeo di Savoia in 1675, to create something long, light and subtle which could be digested. The product was a success, and it later became so popular it entered the daily life of the Torinesi, and soon the whole of Italy.

40. Cakes Without Borders

A Puit d, amour in France is not the same as a Puit d, amour in Mauritius.
An English Madeleine is different to a French Madeleine,
A Greek Yo-yo is different to an Australian Yo-yo,
A Spanish churro donut is different to an English jam donut,
A Portuguese custard tart is different to a Chinese custard tart,
An American muffin is different to an English muffin,
A French yoghurt cake is different from a Greek yoghurt cake
A Sri-Lankan love cake differs from Persian love cake,
A Swiss roulade isn't the same as an English Swiss roll,
Italian Florentina cake isn't the same as an English Florentine gateau.
A Genoese in England is different to a Genoise sponge in France,
An American chiffon cake differs from Japanese cotton cake,
A London cheesecake differs greatly from a New York cheesecake,
Japanese Castella cake is different from Korean Bansuk castella cake,
Chinese Thousand-layer cake is different from French mille–fieulle cake,
Austrian Sacher torte, differs to a Mississippi chocolate mud cake,
Greek Orange olive oil cake differs to an Israel lemon olive oil cake,
Turkish Ek-mek cake is not the same as Chinese egg cake,
Australian Pavlova cake differs from Swedish Pavlova roulade cake
An English tiered wedding cake is different from a Danish stacked
    wedding cake (Kransekage).
A Swedish apple cake is different from a Russian apple cake (Russian
    sharlotka).

A Dutch butter cake (Boterkoek) is different to an English butter pound cake.

German spiced honey cake differs to Croatian honey cake,

Russian Medovik layered honey cake is different to Fijian honey cake,

A Jamaican Black cake is different to a Scottish Black Pudding cake,

Polish Sekacz tree cake differs slightly too Lithuanian sakotis tree cake,

North American dirt cake is different to North American mud cake

Dutch Tom pouce is different to French gateau tom-pouce

Hungarian chimney /funnel cakes are different to Sicilian Cartocci donut cakes,

French meringue "Coque" is different to the Greek "Kok" Othello sandwich cake,

Lebanese Stouf semolina cake is different to Egyptian Basbousa semolina cake,

Greek Ravini lemon coconut cake is different from American lemon coconut chiffon cake,

Columbian dulche de leche milhoja Napoleon cake differs from Argentinian Alfajor Rogel dulche de leche cake

French Napoleon Cake differs from English Nelson Cake

Vinarterta Icelandic layered Xmas cake is different from Italian Iced Xmas Panetonne Cake,

American pineapple upside down cake, differs from Italian plum upside-down cake,

Mexican Tres Leches Cake differs from an English Banoffee pie cake dessert,

Lebanese Baklava cake differs from Turkish and Greek forms of Baklava cake.

In a world of contrast, in a world of difference,

One thing remains the same,

And that is that cake is a unifier, a token, a collective frame,

That binds the human spirit and connects with all asunder,

It encompasses mankind; it enrobes all equality and age,

It defines love, generosity, caring, and a willing for sharing

And more importantly, it puts us all on the same page.

41. Summer Baking

With modern day air conditioning, and the use of refrigeration and freezers, it has made the life of the baker a lot easier than yesteryear. Retarder provers hold doughs in a controlled chilled environment, until timed to commence proving at regulated temperatures.

All in all, baking has become a much easier process in today's world. However, it may be worth noting that the following cautions can be adhered to if so required. The discipline required in summer baking is to keep the products at or below the RDT – required dough temperature.

Examples

1. Colder water in doughs and pastes. (Water can be placed in buckets and fridged overnight)
2. Cooler flour. (Sealed bags of flour can be placed in the cold room overnight, especially if the storeroom is too warm. If too cold, add one bag of ambient temperature flour to one bag of cold flour when mixing doughs)
3. Less yeast is required in bulk dough's during warmer months.
4. Less bread improver – if used – need be added. In fact, it can be completely dismissed during hot weather conditions, but not if the dough is to be frozen and then baked at a later stage.

5. Sour doughs (Pain au Levain) which can contain 2grams of instant yeast to every One Kilo flour, can be completely omitted in summer months.

6. Quicker, shorter mixing times – as the spiral mixer may be warmer than usual, and friction heat will increase.

7. Lower finished dough temperatures, to prevent overactive fermentation. Shorter proving times.

8. Keep yesterday's old dough or pre ferments and sponges in the fridge until mixing times.

9. Aim for smaller batch mixings, as opposed to large mixings, to retain control of the dough temperature.

10. Salt can be increased slightly to control the fermentation process, and to assist in preserving during warmer months.

11. Aim to work at earlier hours, or through the night, when temperatures are cooler than during the day. Aim to have the oven off as early as possible, so as not to increase the temperature of the bake house during daytime, especially towards noon.

12. If using a planetary mixer, this can be placed with attachments overnight into the cool room fridge – if there is one on sight.

13. Keep all fats in the cold room – or in a cool area of the bake house.

14. Dough's can be placed directly into the cold room once mixed, and divided up, if in large bulk. This allows for greater control in working of the dough's as and when required.

15. Use the freezer if applicable as opposed to the fridge to hold all viennoiserie laminated yeasted products during their resting

periods. This provides quicker and more pronounced chilling of the fats – especially if butter is being used – and easier handling properties.

16. Refrigerated marbles are a god – send in summer, but unfortunately not every bakery is lucky enough to have one. Ice bags from the freezer can cool down a metal table or marble slab sufficiently quickly enough, to prepare yeast and paste work in warmer months.

17. Keep all sweet paste and shortbread in the fridge until required. Simply bring to working use by mixing slowly in the spiral or planetary mixer with a hook, to handling use. This is better than placing in a microwave or leaving at ambient temperature to soften up.

18. Only mix the required amounts you need, to keep the paste cold.

19. Puff pastry dough is best prepared the day before and rested in the fridge overnight to obtain maximum chill factor and then laminate with fat the following day.

20. Viennoiserie laminated dough's can also be prepared the day before, to facilitate lamination during warmer weather conditions.

21. Most bakeries use window vents and extractors to retain coolness in the bakery as air conditioning is required for the cooler preparation areas and the shop fronts. It is seldom seen for the oven area to have air-com fitted, so it is important to regulate the heat from the ovens a much as possible. Only have on as and when required, keep the doors closed and the heat inside as much

as possible, and use a fan in the area to help remove the excess heat and retain coolness.

22. Items such as shortbread paste (sweet pastry) can be mixed all in one, as the fat if left out of the fridge overnight, will have become suppler and softer to use. In winter the fat will have to be creamed first with the sugar before adding flour and eggs or at least passed through the oven or microwave to soften.

23. Butter puff pastry detrempe (dough) in Summer can be made by the all in method – flour, salt, soft butter, cold water and white vinegar mixed to a dough, before dividing and scaling and cooling in the fridge overnight. In winter, the butter must be melted first, added to the water and vinegar, mixed and then added to the flour and salt to create the dough.

24. For Bakery, try to work quickly, efficiently and before sunrise, if possible, to eliminate heat rise. Pastry work can be divided up during the day using the fridges/freezers and fans. The heat will always peak around midday to midafternoon, so try to avoid this by working an earlier timetable. All in all, the heat will test your temperament more than the cold. Aim to combat it with every possible conceivable appliance and knowledge.

25. Try to regulate baking times to have the oven turned off when not required and avoid the bake house becoming too hot. This will help to reduce running costs but more importantly assist in creating a more desirable working temperature, atmosphere and ambiance.

26. Remember that Fridges, freezers, and especially walk in cold rooms and freezers, are at their most venerable during the summer months and can become more temperamental with opening, closing and constant entering. Try to maintain door closure or maybe invest in plastic door flaps hung in front of the door to retain coldness and less warmth entering. Avoid unnecessary entering or at last try to condense the number of times required to open the door.

27. Monitor their temperatures twice, three times a day if necessary. A quick glance at the temperature gauge to see how they're performing takes a split second and is worth piece of mind.

Always aim to keep cool

42. Yesteryear

Where are the bread forks of yesteryear?

Where are the dough troughs?

Where are the wooden bread tables?

Where are the serrated bread steel knives?

The bread sliders on kitchen tables

The dough punchers (Hands and feet)

The kitchen bread boards in households

Where is the Bakers benevolent funding?

Where is the baker's union?

Where are the Bakers scholarships?

Where are bakery apprentices?

Where is the Bakers Arms Hotel?

Where are the rice cones for bakery slips and peels?

Where are the rice paper crosses for Hot cross buns?

Where are the rubber jap mats for japonaise bases?

Where are the crystallised violets, rose petals, mimosa balls, and angelica for decoration?

Where are the wooden baking frames for slab cakes?

Where are the barms?

Where is the free compressed yeast handed to customers on request?

Where is the old dough used as bread improver, replaced by powdered chemical pre-mixes?

Where is the malt syrup added to doughs for yeast feed?

Where are the broken biscuits for sale?

Where are the cylindrical "tunnel" loaves?

Where are the Dampers, Clangers and Sally luns?

Where are the 50 and 70 Kilo bags of flour?

Where are the oiled fueled ovens?

Where is the Butter essence?

Where are the balance scales?

Where are the Bakery Reps with their freebies, updates and network links?

Where is the Wednesday half day closing?

Where is the quiet, restful, peaceful, family orientated Sunday closing?

Where is the collective, forged, camaraderie of the Baking Industry?

43. The World Is a Cake

Cakes are predominantly round as is our World.

Today there are square, hexagonal, oblong, and triangular ones, but the overall majority are round.

Round symbolises eternity, it's for that reason most wedding cakes are round, even if couples decide to mimic their own shape and style today. In the end-round will always be round, as round encompasses things, round is the clock, round is wholesome, round is unison, round is evolvement, round is the sun, moon and the planets, round is closeness and security, money and most meal plates.

Round is also marriage, rings and cakes. Wedding cakes were traditionally round, as round symbolised the three rings of wedlock, the engagement ring, the wedding ring and the eternity ring – hence three round tiers.

There is a different round cake for every part of the world, from Sri Lanka to Singapore, from Malta to Mauritius, and from New Zealand to Sweden. Every country has its own unique offering to the World, its statement and identity which sets it apart, but bonds and unites us together. If you wish to see and understand the mechanics or construction of cakes, then take a trip to Germany, and a look at their tortes. If you want to see flair and creativity, then a trip to Italy and Spain.

For clinical precision, Switzerland, and for sheer artistry, then it must be France and Belgium, who are masters at the forefront of our profession.

For sugar crafted masterpieces, there's the UK or South Africa and for pioneering achievement in cake making, look towards the USA and Canada.

Holland, Sweden, Denmark and Norway, have a unique style of cakes, not Germanic or French, but a distinct adaptation off their own modernism to the World. It's flavorsome, stylish and pretty.

Japan is unique with its own cultural pastries, but can emulate any western cake to perfection, and China has wonderful mix of east and west diversity, which can encapsulate the palette. The list is endless, from Black Jamaican cake in the Caribbean, milk cake in India, Honey cake in Israel, baklava in Turkey, and loukoumas in Greece.

It seems unjust and unfair to not account for other countries, and while a list is useful, the beauty of today's technology allows the individual to look and acquire information on search stations on the computer but unfortunately doesn't allow the experience of seeing it in its own setting. This is what makes them special and worth visiting and searching for.

While working in the States, I was employed in a large patisserie which had a contract with the United Nations. Here we were asked to provide a cake for each country's national birthday, and if you check the calendar, it will be seen that there is practically a cake required for nearly every day of the year. It was a wonderful gesture for me to have partaken in – and reminded me that the world could be one large birthday cake.

We decorated each cake with its own national flag, but with the unity of the flag of the United Nations, by keeping them round.

The World is a cake!

44. Charles Louis Fleischmann
(1835-1897)

It's easy within the bakery trade to take items granted, whether its flour, running water ground rock salt. Fresh yeast, Compound yeast, Yeast cake – however it deemed – is another one of these so-called items.

CHARLES FLEISCHMANN

Its readily available, an easy-to-handle block, pre-wrapped and a quick go-to. If it's not around – then there's always instant dried yeast – a compromise or secondary choice.

In today's world of baking – excluding sour dough starters, levains – pre-ferments, natural fermentation – it's worth noting that fresh yeast still rules supreme. The reason being is simply its fresh, it gives better flavour than dried, and it contains moisture and a certain aroma. It contains certain by-products but these are to sustain its shelf life. On the downside – It can decay quickly if not cared for and therefore lose its leavening power – but then it can become a hybrid by using both fresh and dried in a recipe formula.

(In general, it makes sense to use a fresh product over a dried product – unless decaying – and unless there is limited refrigeration or storage space. For example – dried instant yeast is an excellent commodity on merchant shipping / Cruise liners when the delivery times and restocking are limited.)

The big problem is if the prepared product dough is rushed – commonly termed as a "no-time dough". With hot bread shops and quick fermentation – in the forsake of fast food and fast everything – came increased yeast levels – which will activate the dough – but to the detriment of not allowing time for flavour, enzyme breakdown of the starches in the flour and excess gas. All these contribute to indigestion and the common ailment of people complaining of gluten and stomach bloating.

Whereas in the past it was common to use .5% of yeast in a bread formula – overnight sponge and dough – this can and has been increased to 3% in today's breads and 5% in sweetened doughs. Yeast is still required in Bakeries and baking in general – but it needs to be controlled – aided – not rushed – and cared for. It's the great convenience improvisor – and where would we be without it. Which allows me to turn to Charles Louis Fleischmann.

I've mentioned his name on several occasions to fellow bakers – and they remain confused as to who and what I'm talking about. It only when I mention an unknown impressive fact – is it that they connect. The fact being – Charles Fleischmann processed and developed the compressed yeast cake manufacture which is commonly used by most bakers – but more impressively, was that he died the second richest man in the world – after Henry Ford at the time in America. He amassed a huge wealth and fortune – simply by taking living spores from nature and its surroundings and manufacturing this yeast in a manner it could be caked/ blocked/ and sold to the retail market as a convenience product to assist not only professional bakers – but also home bakers too.

We have much to acknowledge and thank him for his pioneering work and commitment – and providing us with what can only be described as a saving grace and a worldly provision. It's hard to put into words the value of his endeavours and achievements.

Of course, we can't get too sentimental in our praise – but we can always play tribute to the man himself, who drove and pushed for the benefit of others. He saw a gap in the market and new it had to be addressed. With this comes credence and for his name's sake – a little fame.

Thank you, Charles Fleischmann.

Charles louis Fleischmann

Hungarian brothers Charles and Max Fleischmann were part of the mid-19th century wave of central European Jews arriving in America, where they settled in Cincinnati and became yeast manufacturers in 1868. Charles had learned the process in in Prague and Vienna, eventually overseeing production on a Nobles estate.

They had searched for a better life in America, and for them that meant making better bread. In an effort to make a better – rising bread they had known in their homeland – the Fleischmann brothers partnered with an American businessman James Gaff to build a yeast plant in Cincinnati, Ohio., It was there that the brothers produced and patented a compressed yeast cake that revolutionised home and commercial baking in the United States and eventually worldwide.

The Fleischmanns family's story echoes the experience of many immigrant Jews who built on their experience of Europe, and using it to fully intergrade into America society,

Without routines to hinder them, innovative business practices bought success. Finally, they used their power to benefit the community and eventually the whole baking sector.

Because of Americas poor quality baked products at the time, the Fleischmanns saw the business opportunity which lay ahead. Soon they were mass producing pressed cakes of yeast and progressing to sales in other states.

Charles himself did hold some production patents in America, but the main steps were invented decades earlier in Vienna. His genius lay not in inventing a new product, but in clever distribution and marketing techniques.

For Charles, delivery of his pressed cakes became much easier in the 1880s with the invention of refrigerated railcars, which thus allowed him the access and time factor to deliver state -wide and eventually the whole of America. Initially compressed yeast could only survive a few days, so reaching customers became his top priority, building a network of production and distribution centres to reach throughout the country.

The company's first major marketing coup came at the 1876 Centennial Exhibition in Philadelphia, where it featured a Vienna model Bakery to demonstrate its product. The fair attracted 10 million visitors, many of whom stopped to sample the delicious bread.

From this, compressed yeast became the preeminent solution for home bakers and impacted production for commercial bakeries too.

With the by – product of yeast production – Charles also added distilled spirits to the company's offerings, using the grain alcohol and adding juniper berries and other botanicals to produce America's first distilled Gin with other hard liquors to follow.

Today Fleischmanns is no longer a Family – owned company. In 1929 the company was merged with Standard Brands. Later Standard Brands merged with Nabisco Brands Inc. in 1981, and in 1986 RJR Nabisco sold Fleischmann company to the Australian company Burns Philip for $130 million dollars.

Eventually Burns Philip sold its yeast business to Associated British Foods in 2004 for US$1.4 billion dollars.

45. The Pastry Chef

Placing different layers, different fillings, different textures, and different colours together can form a cake or dessert but will not necessarily equate to being a Pastry chef, but with creative instinct, imagination, visual interpretation, and a little artistic flair, then the concept of achieving Pastry chef status starts to unfold.

Pastry should be inventive, it should evolve, it should be going in the right direction, but at the same time it should never lose sight of its humble roots. Where pastry chefs came from, trained, initiated themselves, are just as important as to the design and type of pastry they want to prepare, associate with, and propagate within the marketplace.

That hallmark then can slowly become their trademark, a resemblance of themselves, their journey, and their take as to how pastry should be perceived and enjoyed.

Being a pastry chef, it's worth adhering to the following,

1. Uphold your basic training, mentors, your fundamental being as a humanitarian on this planet.
2. Put people before pastry. What good is any cake or dessert – if it was not designed for someone else's enjoyment than your own,
3. Treat those around you as an equal. The total general knowledge of your workforce, or those beside you, exceeds yours.
4. As the pastry chef, you may have more specialised knowledge – but pastry is about life, colour, concepts, social history, movement,

art, design, philosophy, and is a living breathing matter, so it stands to reason that more input and thought process from a wider source, equals more ideas, wisdom and thinking.

5. Be humble – remember all those before you, who worked twice as hard, twice as long, with a lot less for a lot less than you. They gave so you could benefit. Your job is to precipitate this to those under you. Give – don't just take.

6. Don't mock, belittle, or diffuse others, because you don't see them in the same light as yourself. Everyone has something to offer, whether it is a simple recipe, method, idea, or word.

7. Pastry work is a profession, but it's also a life sustaining substance. It's something we consume, to sustain hunger, or sweet cravings, or consume to celebrate an event. How then can you predominate over your goods? Your products are supposed to outshine you – If they don't – you've failed!

8. Any kudos should be associated with your work. If you need "limelight deprivation syndrome" (LDS), then again, you are in the wrong profession.

9. Media pastry chefs are few and far between. Yes, they exist – sometimes due to the fact the media want them to exist for satisfying the public's need to have someone to fill a void, but they are sometimes propelled into this unwittingly. Are they different? -unfortunately not. Like any chef – they are only as good as their team behind them.

10. A pastry chef should always remain true to themselves. It will show in your work, your products, your surroundings, your character, your persona, your purpose in life.

28. Pastry work isn't a sentence of hardship and toil. It's what you make it, how you work it to your benefit, and how you ascertain the self-satisfaction and fulfilment from it, plus how you share it.

29. The nature of the pastry chef is something that is seldom or ever discussed. Where you were raised, your background, your upbringing, schooling, grooming, family, will all play an infinite role in how you conduct yourself, how and why your thought process is, your values, your perceptions, your decisions, and your interpretation of almost everything that surrounds you.

30. Now place all that on a plate – divided by all other pastry chefs, and you will see the comparison, but also the differential. Yes, we are bound, but we are also free agents. We can put ourselves on the plate – to some degree – and there are few jobs like this in the World today.

31. The country you were born can play a major role in your aspiring to become a pastry chef. Many may disagree, but being born or raised in the European continent, where pastry is considered part of everyday life, with very high standards, can assist in the interpretation of the job role. That doesn't mean to say that a person interested in a career in pastry born elsewhere can't make it, it's just that they will have to try and pursue it more intensely to achieve the same recognition.

32. Pastry has a strong connotation with European roots, where the profession has been handed down generation to generation. It has fixed methods and products that have stood the test of time and consequently been mimicked elsewhere. Their strong convictions of their products is also a test to their belief core, that this is how pastry should look, taste, eat and be admired. It is extremely difficult to sometimes to try and sway chefs who have trained this way, but with a little time, travel, open –mindedness, awareness, discussion, they slowly conceive that there is so much more to pastry, than one country. Again, I go back to the initial statement, that where you're born, has a huge influence on your outlook, but doesn't in any way confirm or prevent you adapting other new and varied techniques and guises to the world of pastry work.

33. There was a period when i felt personally that I had been born in the wrong country to pursue the profession of a pastry chef, and that I have emulated a lot from those predecessors who in some cases have emulated it from their predecessors. Pastry in the UK is a mishmash of continental influences, global diversity, American and commonwealth input and Anglo – Saxon and Celtic tradition. The Victorian era brought the biggest revolution in the change of pastry with French chefs being brought to work in London, such as Careme, Escoffier to name, and thus changed the concept of pastry as we know it today. The only problem was that if you were born elsewhere in the UK, you were not privy to any of these ideas, movements, designs, concepts and recipes etc.

34. Entering the world of pastry without any concept of what it meant to be – can be a huge daunting task.

35. Pre – conceived ideas of Pastry chefs, can be the exact opposite of pastry chefs from elsewhere. How to merge, marry and unite them depends on how flexible you are as an individual.

36. Emulating others prompted me to call this work "Mock cuisine" as I've aptly named it. Here I followed suite on everything that was regarded as the norm, the name of the dish, the correct title, the correct procedure, the recipe, format, workflow and presentation.

37. I was never myself in the early years. I struggled to find myself – find a job where I could put myself on a plate, where I didn't have to contrive to the same old perpetual onslaught of the daily grind and thought process. To break free, was an immense feeling of freedom. It can come at any time or stage in your career, preferably earlier than later. This then gives you confidence, self-belief and the

38. knowing that you were meant to be a pastry chef -, irrelevant of where, who, what why or when.

39. Pastry chefs must be free - – It's in their nature!

46. RDT Required Dough Temperature

Why are certain doughs marked at a particular required finished temperature? E.g. – 28C.

RDT can also be referred to as FDT (finished dough temperature) but are of the same meaning.

Why is dough not at 24C or 34C.? – How is this temperature arrived at?

There are many factors which will determine a required dough temperature-or finished dough temperature. They all need to be considered before commencing work. They are as follows,

1. Time allowed (your given working time)
2. Is the dough a "time" dough, or a "no time" dough?
3. Fermentation BFT, or overnight sponge and dough.
4. Temperature of the bake house / room temperature, air temperature.
5. Is the dough to be baked once moulded or left in the fridge overnight.
6. Seasons – (Winter cold) – (Summer – Hot).
7. Mixing times, friction heat incorporated and length of mixing times.
8. The quantity of the dough, large batch or small batch

9. Bakery constraints – Space, Hands, Racks, Oven's capacity, workload.
10. Shaping / pleating-braiding/moulding, garnishing – all requires time.
11. Wet proving or dry proving.
12. Addition of pre-ferments, old dough, soakers, additional ingredients, natural starters, and their temperatures.
13. Most Italian breads aim for a finished dough temperature of 27C. This gives a certain indication of their breads, but if for example there is excessive work involved in preparing and shaping, then most bakers aim for a lower RDT.
14. Normally NTD (No time dough's) are fished around 27-28 C, whereas time doughs are much cooler at around 24 C. Doughs made by the ADD system – (activated dough development) tend to have a finished dough temperature of around 31C, due to the friction heat of a high-speed mixer.
15. By allowing a dough to achieve the desired RDT – you are allowing yourself greater control of the dough against all the above elements., but more importantly allowing the dough to obtain the correct fermentation which leads to the desired finished look and texture.
16. Overactive dough's (too hot) will be sticky and difficult to handle and mould. On the opposite side of the scale, dough's too cold will not ferment correctly and be under ripe, or green as known in the trade.
17. The RDT or FDT are essential in bakery to maintain consistent daily products and end results

47. Half Baked

Cookies in shop windows,
Look as though they've been there a decade or two,
Reheated yesterday's croissants,
Made to look as though baked and new,
Dummy cakes on shelves, with dust to decorate or detract,
Shop windows stained, murky, unpolished, no vent to extract.

Cakes placed on cake boards, soiled with chocolate,
Underneath fingerprint markings, an added unfortunate,
Chocolate goods weeping due to refrigeration too high,
Losing their sheen, glow, an unattractive appeal contributed,
Cakes not rotated daily, platters not redressed,
Selling goods that are deflated, dated, and demeaning our quest.

Products not uniform, decorations not neat,
Some trays full, others incomplete,
Paper and cassette cases limp and tired,
Others disfigured, so not really required,
Prices and products not labelled or priced,
Confused customers, bemused so – not exactly enticed.

No sneeze guards – placed to protect daily bakes,

No product list to engage customers likes or distastes,

No temperature logs, no mission – vision statement on show,

No cheerful Hello, no soulful glee, no ambient temperature flow,

Just the usual unrelinquished Hi, no smile attired, a quick goodbye,

Motions, apathy, and quick consents, addressed with a usual big sigh.

Ununiformed staff – Servers not correctly attired,

Un-mopped floors – no cleaning companies or agents hired.

Closing the shop up to finalise the day,

Leaving cakes and pastries still on display,

Not bothering to empty the racks or cake and cookie cabinet,

Or covering with cloths as in the past, an accustomed accurate.

Unwashed prongs, cake tongues and servers left unoccupied,

Clothes and tea towels not soaked overnight; no sanitiser applied,

Garbage bins not removed daily – no deep cleaning accounted for,

The routine of being in control – procedures and stock the major core,

Because if not -it's the stigma of being here -but not being accountable,

And the term "Half Baked" becomes synonymous and insurmountable.

48. One Direction

We've gone from,
Bakery to Cakery,
Cake parlour to Wedding cake studio,
Soda milk bar to Gelati bar,
Hot bread shops to Cupcake shops,
Classical cuisine to Conceptual theme cuisine,
Chef Confiseur to Jellyologist, Chocologist and Marshmallowist,
Macaroons to Macarons,
Macarons to Macalongs
Donuts to Cronuts,
Muffins to Cruffins,
Brownies to Crownies,
Cookies to Brookies
Chocolate éclairs to Multi garnished and decorated éclairs,
Commercial grains to ancient grains,
Caged eggs to Free range eggs,
Purchased commercial yeast to natural yeast,
Hydrogenated fats to Mycrya cocoa butter fats,
Fast food meals to slow food products,
Traditional cakes to Vegan, gluten free and sugar free cakes,
White sliced bread loaves, to seeded grained and naturally fermented loaves,

Quick no timed activated developed doughs to slow timed matured sour doughs,

Chocolate lamingtons to Lamington eclairs,

Black forest cakes to green forest cakes

High teas to flavoured teas,

Apple pies to whoopee pies,

Automatic bread mixing to autolyse bread mixing,

Flour used on baking tables, to simply canola spray on tables, moulding machines, and baking trays, for commercial doughs,

Baking chocolate to chilli chocolate,

Chocolate mousse with eggs to chocolate mousse with water, (Ref: Heston Blumenthal)

Simple caramel syrup to Goats milk caramel, beetroot caramel and whey caramel,

Spiced hot cross buns to lemon myrtle / spelt / chocolate hot cross buns,

Gum Arabic and tragacanth to Xavier and guar gums,

Plexiglass chocolate moulds to polycarbonate moulds,

Cotton piping bags to thermo nylon and disposable bags,

Tempered chocolate to roasted chocolate soil, crumble, garnish,

Freeze stable products to freeze dried products,

Layered laminated paste work, to layered pastries and cake slices,

Copy cake iced imagery to rice paper edible imagery,

Dessert trolleys to dessert bars,

Dairy ice cream to Keffir ice, Yoghurt ice and Burnt milk ice creams,

Fruit paste confections to fruit leather decorations,

Portioned cakes and desserts to individual plated desserts,

Sweet dessert menus to savoury dessert options,

Puddings with sauce, to self-saucing puddings,

Bavarois and mousse desserts to Cremeaux and Aeromousse desserts,

Hand whisks and planetary machines for aerating cream, to siphon with cartridges, and countertop refrigerated whipping machines,

Edible show pieces to edible installations,

Intermediate course sorbets, to plated pre-desserts,

Nappage and clear glaze to metallic and mirror glaze,

Gooseberry fruits to kiwi berry fruits,

Crystallised and piped flowers, to edible micro herbs, plants and flowers,

Starch imprint moulds for fondant and liqueur chocolates, to silicon flexi pat moulds,

Baking on silpat mats, to forming cakes and desserts in silicon moulds,

Cake hoops to extendable frames,

Cake decorating to cake styling,

Decorating with royal icing to decorating with moulded Isomalt syrup,

Metal piping tubes to microwavable plastic tubes,

Greasing and flouring baking tins/trays, to canola spray greasing trays and tins,

Parchment paper to Silpain mats,

Caraway seeded goods to quinoa/chia seeded goods,

Soft fondant icing work to rolled fondant icing cakes,

Degustation tasting to degustation menus,

Savoury canapés to dessert canapés,

Sugar baking to sugar-free baking,

Sweet desserts to savoury desserts,

Brioche a Tete, to laminated brioche goods,

Biscuits to cookies, Butter cake to Mud cake,

Carrot cake to red velvet cake,

Lumberjack cake to Hummingbird cake,

Iced wedding cake to Naked wedding cake,

Engagement cakes to Gender reveal cakes,

Drying out goods in the oven, to drying out goods in the humidifier,

Imported produce to searching local produce,

Mass farmed products to ethically organic grown goods,

Frozen sorbets to nitrogen chilled and blended ices,

Three coloured angel cake to seven layered rainbow cakes,

Desiccated coconut for cakes to coconut cream for ganache,

Covering up excess goods to vacuum packing excess goods,

Cutting cakes by hand to water laser cutting modules,

Kopycake machines for edible imaginary, to edible rice paper transfers,

Raw sugar to raw cakes,

Cupcakes to mug cakes,

Scratch baking to Pre-mix Baking

Kitchen chefs to Garden chefs,

Mimosa balls to candy popping balls,

Tulip tuille cases to spaghetti nest tuille cases,

Terrines to verrines,

Caramel cages to isomalt vases,

Baked sponges to microwaved sponges,

Fresh fruits to freeze dried fruits,

Glace fruits to dehydrated fresh fruit slices,

Hand brushing to air brushing, (egg washing, glazing, spraying, finishing)

Mainstream honey to rooftop honey,

Cotton piping bags to disposable piping bags,

Vanilla beans to Tonka beans,

Lemon juice in desserts to lemon jus on desserts,

Stacked desserts to deconstructed desserts,

Soaking and sandwiching cakes together, to layering, formatting and texturizing cakes,

Essence to extracts, liquid flavouring to compounds,

Rice puffs to Souffletine,

Cornflakes to Fieulletine,

Gum tragacanth to CMC,

Traditional genoise to emulsified Genoese,

Tiramisu to Strawberrymisu and Beeramisu,

Lemon tart to Lime gin and tonic tart,

Dry ice presentations to nitrogen iced cream desserts,

Drop scones to drip cakes,

Bubble sugar decoration to edible cellophane wrapping and balloons,

Filigree and finer lace piping to stencil mats with sugar-veil premix,

Chocolate teardrops to chocolate drip cakes

Coffee, mocha, espresso flavouring to Matcha green tea flavouring compositions,

Fair trade to free trade,

Cooking foodstuffs on the stove top, to preparing and cooking with a thermo mix,

Copper sugar boilers and bowls, to Innox stainless steel pans with aluminium sandwiches,

Gas stoves to Induction stoves,

Clear Gel glaze to coloured mirror glazes

Meat pies to Plant based pies

Rainbow cakes to Rainbow bagels

Choux baked stalagmites to Choux filled Bombes

Gluten free baking to Keto Baking

Gluten Free labelling to Gluten friendly advertising

Battenburg chequered cakes to Barrel shaped drip cakes

Donuts and Muffins to hybrid Duffins

Croissants and waffle to Croffle – croissant waffle toasted in a waffle machine

Plain flan rings to micro perforated flan rings – (for better colour/crust formation in baking)

Honey joy Cakes to popsicle cakes

Placing VOL in choux pastry to placing Craqulin on choux pastry.

Microwaves to Micro herbs

Chocolate chip cookies to Funfetti cookies

Decorating cakes with writing – to simply applying cake toppers.

Retail Bakeries to Boutique Bakeries,

Scratch baking to Botanical baking.

49. Bakers Scones

Scones are scones!

But Bakers scones aren't simply chemically aerated, or lemonade activated.

Bakers' scones are simple and modest – they're baked in in a bakery – and not necessarily with a pre-mix or packet ingredients.

Bakers would normally use the same machines to mix a scone dough as the previous bread dough had been mixed in – this leaving the yeast bacteria to be combined into the scone mix.

This acts as a panary aeration combined with the chemical aeration from the baking powder.

Some bakers would throw a nugget of fresh yeast into a chemically aerated scone mix – to provide that extra lift and use slightly more tepid water or milk.

Other bakers would add a small addition of bun dough scraps or bread dough scraps to the scone mix – again adding additional lift and volume, and lightness.

Sour dough starter (mother) or sour dough trimmings can also be included into this regime to pre-empt what has already been stated.

In addition to this, retail bakers have been known to sell chemically aerated fruit scones – egg washed – adjacent to plain baker's scones which were simply dusted with flour. Thus, dividing the two in separate categories provides the customers with more choice and preference.

A proper scone should neither be too biscuit or too muffin type -but should fall somewhere between the two.

Bakers' scones allow for a lighter, more voluminous product and give credence to the baker's profession. Scones have been domesticated and appear anywhere and at any time. They are conceived as part of daily bakes – and for that reason are considered the norm -however they're produced.

There is no consensus of how they should be produced, with simplicity and ease of workload at the forefront in their method. However, Bakers scones will have a longer shelf life, will remain softer, and will be to some degree guaranteed to rise.

Double aeration equates to double success.

Recipe For Bakers Scone

Ferment for 30 minutes	Dough	
150 ml Water	1250 g Bakers Flour	200g Caster Sugar
60g Fresh Yeast	60g Baking Powder	560ml Milk.
125g Bakers Flour	60g Whole Egg	125g Sultana (optional)
	200g Butter	Lemon and Vanilla Flavour

50. You Know you're a Baker When...

1. One hour before seven a.m. – equals two after.
2. You work with flour -not in it.
3. The burns on your forearms are the only reference needed on your resume.
4. You're the best applicant to qualify for the position of a formulator – (used by pharmaceutical companies in preparing and weighing ingredients in the manufacture of medicinal products)
5. Flour is your weapon of choice -your poison-your friend-your go to-your financial investment.
6. You have clear roads while driving early morning to work.
7. Your razor blades somehow seem designed for scoring loaves, rather than shaving.
8. You believe ensuring your hands seems more important than insuring your car.
9. Bread is your democracy, your human rights resource, your faith, and your legacy to mother earth.
10. Physicality, manual labour, hands on approach and practicality are the order of the day / night.
11. Your calculator somehow seems more appropriate in your pocket than a smart phone.

12. Scaling is your answer to meditation, hand moulding your therapeutic personal exercise, and freshly baked goods your aromatherapy healing process.
13. Time and temperature are your two most important elements in the workplace – after coffee and the radio.
14. Scrapers are a necessity, scales are part of the furniture, oven mitts your dress code.
15. You accept gluten free, nut free, dairy free, egg free, lactose free, egg free, sugar free -as your daily dilemma – to obtain a hassle-free day.
16. You realise that your hands are the most important piece of equipment in the workplace.
17. Hand depositing, handing up, pleating and shaping are performed possibly quicker than by a machine.
18. You'll never have to worry about your own birthday cake!
19. Checking out bottoms – is a daily ritual during baking.
20. Weighing, measuring, mixing, dividing, scaling, moulding, pleating, scoring is not perceived as work – they're simply applied bodily movements.
21. You've mistaken Pilates with pies and Lattes, Yoga for Yuzu, and referred to aerobics as Gluten free bics.
22. Bischoff, Banoffee, and Burnt milk, are your B -Plan – while salted caramel, red velvet, lemon marshmallow, rainbow and chocolate mud remain you're A-Game.

23. Your body clock, alarm clock, retarder and oven clock are all somehow synchronised.

24. You classify as being Nocturnal

25. Your French sticks, German Rye, Vienna bloomers, Scandinavian crisp breads and Irish Soda Bread – allow you credibility on the World stage.

26. Your daily press is performed on your BDM – not on the bench.

27. The term "Friday night jobber" has been erased from your vocabulary and replaced with prover retarder.

28. Your BDM moulder, French stick moulder and tart/pie moulder – are instinctively attached to your arms – and are your middle shoulder.

29. The Bakers Arms – just happen to be your favourite Pub / Hotel eatery.

30. Your Custard Apple refers to a Danish pastry – not a tropical fruit.

31. You revert from using the "C" word as much as possible (Christmas) – as it conveys more work, more hours, more cleaning, more headaches.

32. You opt for a partner in life – who isn't gluten intolerant.

33. Unlike Tradies – your call out fee – is free!

34. Walking around with your arms folded, your hands on your hips, or your hands in your pockets – are not a condition of employment, and very seldom actually possible.

35. Vegan, Coeliac, Diabetic, makes you conscious of your role in protecting society.

36. Slow food has always been on your agenda – it's your fifth ingredient-(Time).

37. Allergies, intolerances, and sensitivities are a required benchmark with all your baked products.

38. Reliability, Consistency, Fortitude – is all part of your DNA.

39. Your mother (Natural starter) is fed every day, besides being nurtured, assessed, pampered, and continuously cared for.

40. You know the difference between flour and dandruff.

41. Your attire isn't simply bakery whites-it's your flannel oven mitts, your piping bag with French cuffs, and your floured Croc shoes with polka dot socks.

42. You fashion your hair in a head bun, with pride.

43. You grow immune to customers who seemingly look for products you don't have, seemingly question products you do have, and seemingly question "Is it Fresh "!!!!!

44. You know that Beer is great food for feeding your Rye starter dough – as well as refreshing your palette.

45. Low carb days and diets aren't – and never will be part of your repertoire.

46. The flour scoop is removed before topping up the flour bins – it just helps!!!

47. Your puff pastry gets more resting periods than you.

48. When Bischoff reminds you of a Day-off.

49. Being late for work is inexcusable, underweight bread unacceptable, and burning products basically a sin.

50. You shudder and gasp at the price of commodities, resources, equipment – but you know your customers smiles cost nothing.

51. You accept that butter, almonds, chocolate are all considered luxury and expensive products – but remain integral to the profession.

52. You've accepted that naked cakes, same sex wedding cakes, gender reveal cakes, and divorce cakes will be requested and expected – without discriminative agendas.

53. The numbers 13, 365, 95 are locked in your memory, (Baker's dozen, days of the year, internal temperature of baked bread)

54. You know texture of fats comes before temperature of fats when laminating pastes.

55. Your fondant kettle somehow seems more active than your electric kettle.

56. You acquire Asbestos hands

57. Your freshly baked muffins on the removal of the oven – are a definite "Good Morning "to you.

58. You know that "Patience "is the most important ingredient in Baking.

59. Cleaning your oven mitts – somehow gets more precedence than cleaning your shelves.

60. Success for you is a baked French meringue cake – "Success"

51. The Power of Pastry

Pastry has the power to encapsulate,
It has direct symmetry.
It has an obscure movement.
It has the magic to allure.

The stance to bewitch.
The beauty to enthrall.
The taste to succumb too.
It has the strength to construct.
Yet the fragility to crumble

Pastry has the finesse to enrich.
It has glamour to grace.
It has the desirability to dazzle.
And the evocativeness to tantalise.

It has the richness to bequeath.
It has the splendor to speak.
It has the science to unravel.
It has the chemistry to unearth.

It has the pleasure to promote.

It has the opulence to enthrall.

The sweetness to seduce.

And the colour to mesmerise.

Pastry has the power -It's in your hands, for you to withhold,

Its aesthetics, history, acknowledgment, and credibility left for you to unfold.

52. Bakery and The Foreign Legion

The 'Legion Étranger" as its commonly known in France is the Foreign Legion.

This is the elite fighting force of France -who always are the first battalion to march down the "Champs Elysée" in Paris during the commemorations of Bastille Day – 14th July each year.

The battalion is unique – as it accepts conscripts from anywhere in the World. The requirements for enrolment are simple – "Ignorance is strength".

Joining the Foreign legion, you will be told to leave your head at the door. There is no room for individuality and thinking. They will feed you, beat you and train you like dogs. If the legion is an awesome war machine, it is with this sort of philosophy in mind.

It is a form of taught courage, ultimate discipline, which is drilled into you – and you'll have a much easier time once you accept this.

Bakery for me became my Foreign Legion.

Crossing the English Channel and entering France aged 26, I felt I had signed up to a unique legion, different language, culture, mannerisms, work ethic, and discipline. I was assigned to work amongst Algerians, Moroccans, Tunisians, Senegal's from North Africa and French speaking nations, and amongst Belgians, Japanese, and any other nation that springs to mind. They were tough, hardworking, fearsome and disciplined by the authoritarian way the business was run.

Timekeeping was absolute – if you arrived later than 3-30am – the doors would remain locked until 5-30 am when the delivery vans arrived. That required you to stand outside in the cold for two hours -pending on the weather and owning transport.

It was a tough, harsh and disciplined environment where the factory (Laboratoire) was on the outskirts of Paris in a suburb (Banlieue) called Courbevoie. Because the business was reputable and amongst the four top pastry shops in Paris – there was little room for negligence, apathy or laziness.

We worked hard, quietly, focused, diligently -that's all, I can recall. I ended up forging an inner strength, a tougher backbone and a resilience second to none. Besides being beaten a few times and punched and hit, and struggling to understand French – plus trying to let others understand myself – I remained true to the course as I was amongst the best of the best in France.

I was seeing, learning, adapting, acquiring and climbing. I was paid the minimum wage in France -the SMIG (Salaire minimum interprofessional garanti) – which kept me alive, fed and watered and enough to get by on without spending.

(– the basic minimum wage to exist. Your wealth came from being allowed to work in an established renowned business in the heart of Paris. How you regarded this wealth or dealt with that – was up to the individual)

The code was simple – stay on top or drop.

The call was simple – be tough – be ready – be switched on – be prepared – be focussed and get ready to be undermined if at fault.

The job didn't accept prisoners – you worked hard – and all I remember after five years was being incredibly privileged to have had the opportunity – and not lose it.

Did it have any connotations to the Foreign Legion?

Remarkably so.

The foreign legion accepts anyone from anywhere – refuges – migrants -prisoners-drifters-losers-, lowlifes, and breaks all discretions, disorders, and discrimination boundaries – holding democracy as a core value. It might be authoritarian in its manner – but it fights for freedom, justice, comradeship, dependency, life.

Bakery is democratic, it has no social class barriers – its food for all sundries.

Bakers wear white caps – as do the foreign legion.

They struggle and fight for recognition as bakers do to retain their dignity and standing.

Their core values are no different from the daily requirements of baking.

Bread – the first roll call of the day-the initial start-up – the commencement of the day. The legion being the first to march to uphold Frances "Egalite, Liberte, Fraternite" (Equality, Liberty, Fraternity).

This reflects the baking industry too. Democratic, and libertarian values depict what bakery stands for.

France is the language of food – Bread although not invented in France -has become their quest for refinement and upholding its value and recognition in society worldwide.

Patisserie is unique in France. It became their hallmark for finesse, creativity, drive, vision and notability. Nothing has surpassed their quest globally to be the best of the best.

Foreign legion – Bakery – The epitome of courage, strength and devotion to duty.

It would be wrong to assume that the Foreign Legion and Bakery are identical – but there are many similarities. Prisoners are taught bakery in prison – as a form of rehabilitation., plus being able to prepare themselves for employment on finalising their served time.

Many bakeries will employ those who are willing to work/fight, as there are seldom few who are keen to work nights, unsociable hours, weekends, public holidays etc.

Creed, colour, language barrier is irrelevant – if the candidate is prepared to work – is able bodied – and is reliable.

Again, it familiarises itself with the Legion. Their motto is "Honneur et Fidelite" (Honour and Fidelity) and "Legio Patria" (The Legion is our Fatherland) are the crucible identity of the Foreign Legion.

The Legionnaires Code of Honour – also reflects bakery, in the sense the Legion never abandons its men. It specifies, once again – "In combat, you will act without passion and without hatred, you will respect the vanquished enemies, you will never abandon your dead, your wounded or your arms". This commitment goes well beyond combat.

Bakery never abandons anyone -people abandon bakery.

It never fails to protect and nourish its clientele, wherever they come from – the rich – the poor – the homeless.

Passion/hatred are disclaimers in the bakery field – as there is no individual favouring, no segregation, no disparity, no neglect.

We are uniformed. proud, courageous, and durable, we use our hands, feet and minds to win the day. We are out of site and out of mind – but we are present. Our code is to honour our brethren, supply their needs, and do so daily.

We are taken for granted, underpaid, underrepresented, undervalued. And in some cases, not even regarded as a trade.

We are expected to perform like water running from a tap, rotate like blades on a wind farm, and shine like the rays of the Sun.

Our duties are bound by a higher presence than ourselves.

53. Charles Joughin

The name may sound unfamiliar, the importance of little value, and the relevance of whatsoever.

But here lies an interesting if not fascinating insight to a person to whom should not be forgotten. It's seldom or non-existent to find a Baker to whom you can look up to and forge as an Icon amongst the Bakery / pastry world, yet so little is known of him and with sadly such little interest.

For the record, Charles Joughin was employed by the white star line as the Chief Baker on the RMS Titanic. Born in Birkenhead, England on the 3rd of August 1878, he first went to sea aged 11 years old and became the chief baker on various white star line steamships, notably aboard the Olympic, Titanic's sister ship.

Charles was 22 Years old when he became a Head Baker and was 33 Years old when he joined the Titanic – again as the Head Baker. He had 14 crew in the bakery of the Titanic, two confectioners and one Vienna Baker. Most had worked together on the Olympia before joining the Titanic.

Charles being the Head Baker had access to yeast-and therefore could brew alcohol as well as bake bread.

The Titanic's maiden voyage was sadly also its final voyage. Fortunately for Charles, he survived the sinking unlike many of the 1400 others who perished. Although Charles survived, it was his tenacity and endurance to save others that made him special, plus the fact he was technically the last survivor to leave the RMS Titanic, being on the stern end 150 feet above sea level, before it descended like an elevator into the depths of the Atlantic.

During the evacuation of the ship as it sank, he was responsible for throwing more than fifty deck chairs into the icy cold waters to save others. Charles woke up the other bakers on off duty, to get bread and biscuits sent to the lifeboats and aid those in peril. He is noted as literally throwing women and children into lifeboats, especially women who were reluctant to leave the ship, and using his brute force to save them.

He himself went into the icy-cold water by clambering to the stern rail at the back of the ship, and he literally rode the titanic into the sea like an elevator being the last person on the Titanic to enter the water, where he paddled and treaded water for two hours before eventually clambering into a lifeboat before being rescued by the RMS Carpathia and having only suffered swollen feet.

Having consumed alcohol before the ship went down; it prevented his body from the hypothermia kicking in, by slowing down heat loss and prolonging survival in cold conditions. Charles Joughin survived through a combination of initiative, luck and alcohol, but also endurance in the face of disaster. He saved himself, but he was the hero baker who saved many lives that night, and it's for that sole reason his name should not be forgotten and should be an enduring light for all bakers.

He died at the age of 78 on the 9th ^{of} December 1956 in Paterson, New Jersey, USA.

Gone but not forgotten.

54. Time

Your only enemy is the clock rotating,
Never anticlockwise, never terminating,
You'd think you could beat it, somehow get on top,
How do you control it, without getting it to stop?

It seems a futile battle, a difficult one to achieve,
So, acquiring time management allows you that reprieve.
Assessing what's important and what must come first,
Are priorities to consider if we are to avoid the worst?

It's possible to acquire more money, but never more time,
So, understanding this predicament, makes wasting it a crime,
Time is a precious commodity, every second of every day,
It's even more important than money – if you see it that way.

The clock was invented by man – no need for sun or moon,
It was their way of control, timing -, keeping us in a cocoon,
But time can deprive you, if believing there's 24hrs in a day,
Because then our lives are steered by the clocks constant display.

What is important in baking, is time and temperature,
Whether summer or winter, it's accepting the law of nature,
Therefore, we need to quantify its relevance and accept its call,
As time waits for no one – no matter how fast you're of the wall.

Time isn't a component, nor something you must wear on wrists,
Time shouldn't dictate your life, as it seems that's how it consists,
Time is a gift, like breath – an energy force that circles our life,
Time is an endless faculty that shouldn't be allowed to deprive.

"Time is money – but can money buy time"?
Duncan 2010.

55. Another Book

Another book on cupcakes, another book on madeleines,

Another book on whoopee pies and another on baked donut rings,

Another book on mastering the art of baking, plus one on bars and slices,

Another book on cookies and biscuits, with additional ones for decorated iced guises.

Another book on retro cakes, competition cakes, favourite cakes and vintage cakes,

Another book on simplified baking, with another book on acquiring decorating traits,

Another book to arouse, stimulate and motivate your inner baking desires,

Another book to broaden your recipe collection, so that your passion never tires,

Another book on mastering baking art, another on acquiring new decorating skills,

Another book on tips, technique and trade, with baking bibles added to the overkill,

Another book on cooking with chocolate, another on preparing patisserie at home,

Another book on macarons, iced gelato, pies and tarts, and jellies and sugar foam,

Another Book

Another book on kids' cakes, foolproof cakes, mug cakes, party cakes, mini cakes too,

Another book on vegan bakes, gluten free bakes and extreme bakes to name just a few,

Another book on paleo bakes, indulgent bakes, and whatever can sustain your appetite,

Another day, another book, with sadly no end in sight to this continuing ongoing plight.

Help us please.

56. Fondant Icing

Royal icing sounds very regal,
Water icing – as though it comes from a tap,
Butter icing sounds very rich and calorific,
And American icing – possibly made with measured cups.
But fondant icing!!!!
Sounds very French, and like "Pomme Fondant".

Fudge icing frosting is a cupcake favourite
Cream cheese icing is red velvets best friend,
Honey glaze icing for Donuts and Fritters,
Chocolate glaze icing with honey and butter –sets with a sheen,
But fondant icing!!!!
This must be tempered – like Couverture chocolate.

Rolled sugar paste icing for celebration cakes
Snow sugar / Donut sugar icing for an all-day Bakes,
Parfait icing – a mix of butter cream and fudge frosting,
Sacher icing – for the most famous chocolate cake of all,
But Fondant icing!!!!
The Bakers / Confectioners favourite, and most popular of all.

Fondant Icing to a bakery – is like a dressing to a salad,
It's the one icing that rules supreme, that conjures, controls, delivers,
It adds, it accompanies, and it lifts, accentuates and finishes all in one,
It colours, bonds, and can flavour addressed to the purveyors' requirements,
And if worked correctly, will apply a finish as to whatever is required.

It can be thinned and translucent, allowing it to set and dry,
It can be feathered, marbled, spun, coated or piped,
It can be used to make butter – cream, rolled fondant, caramel coating,
It can be heated and cast into moulds to crystallise and set,
It can be added to fruit purees to sweeten and thicken as a sauce,

No bakery / Pastry shop or confectioners would be seen without it,
It surpasses all other icings – it knows its place and never predominates,
It simply a cooked syrup that's creamed to an opaque mass,
Once produced in house – but now purchased as a convenience product,
Purchased medium, soft, or extra soft – pending on its role required.

It can also be purchased coloured and flavoured to ease the workload,
And in days gone by – was produced in a powdered form (Fondex),
But remember – Fondant must be cared for, scraped down after use,
Surface skin soaked and moistened, before use, temperature gauged,
And fed with a simple syrup preferably, (not water) – to extend and add gloss.

Fondant, respected for its simplicity and uniqueness – the icing extraordinaire.

Tempered Fondant

Not too hot – or it will crystallise

Not too cold – or it won't set

Not too thick – or it won't spread or pour.

Not too thin – or it won't coat or hold its shape

57. Micky

Mice love Bakeries, for them its common ground,
You might not see them, but they're hiding in and around,
They're active on the run, looking for every little morceau,
Scraps or crumbs you've left, from bread, buns, fried churro.

Micky is not interested in your fears or dislikes,
Because Micky is on the prowl, morning and nights,
Micki's interests lie in the place left untidy, unclean,
And Micky will claim any items – raw, cooked or unseen.

Micky is an adventurer, clambering heights unimaginable,
Micky doesn't have routine, because that's not negotiable,
Micky lives on the edge – without taking up too much space,
And Micky can hide in places – that's difficult to find or trace.

Micki's intentions are very clear and straight forward,
Food is for consumption, where left around, unrecorded,
Micky is not concerned about deep cleaning or hygiene,
And pest control-it's a game to dodge, remain unforeseen.

Mice are rodents – and naturally rodent have no rules,
They'll entertain on anything – leaving a trail of stools,
They're renowned on leaving a trail of devastation, detest,
Because Micky has no woes, allowing to run their quest.

It's simply a battle of attrition – Micky against the World,
And Micky doesn't like the bakery cats– tails lying curled,
But it's a way of saying goodbye – you're not required here,
Micky must remain unseen – and then our path is clear.

58. Facts and Myths of Sourdough

Fact – Sour dough is sour!

Sourdough in general has a subtle hint of sourness to a strong sour tang. The term "Sourdough" normally used in bread making refers to "natural yeast cultures" which can be used to produce many types of bread, including those do not sour at all.

The term sourdough doesn't necessarily refer to the flavour but refers to the process of souring or fermenting bread dough. The sourness can be tamed by manipulating the sourdough starter and dough to produce bread that suits the overall customer's requirements.

Fact – Sourdough is the oldest leavened bread around!

Sourdough has been around for thousands of years, although its popularity has recently gone through a renaissance and been rekindled. Sourdough doesn't rely on commercially produced yeasts and, but a mixture of flour and water creating wild yeasts.

Fact – Sourdough cultures have been created through blessed water and even horse manure!

Although contrary to believe, and maybe hard to acknowledge, horse manure in times gone by was the perfect bacteria receptive when mixed with crushed grain and water to create a mother / natural starter for bread.

In Greece, they believe is that blessed water from the church, with a basil leaf placed inside, and then fed with crushed grain, will provide and create a "divine intervention" starter dough.

Although there are many ways, products and factors used to create natural starter dough, the two mentioned above, provide the most intriguing of methods.

Fact – Sourdough is good for you!

According to studies, sourdough acts as a pre-biotic, allowing the fibre to feed the good bacteria in the gut.

Myth – Only Spring /Filtered water can produce a Sourdough starter!

Chlorinated tap water – which includes fluoride-, should be perfectly acceptable to create a sour dough culture – if guided correctly, at the correct temperatures and timings to build a strong mature starter for sourdough bread. Although frowned upon by some, because of the chlorine content, it is possible to achieve an active starter over a period /day with tap water.

Tank water (rainwater) could also be used and is still preferred over tap water to make the sourdough in certain sourdough bakeries, but tap water has seldom failed, and if used at the correct temperature and quantities, is fine.

Myth – Organic flour must be used to feed a natural sourdough starter!

Although organic flour still retains the germ, which is the life source of the grain, it can aid to generate reproduction and the fermentation process – but this is no different than adding a small quantity of rye flour with commercial wheat flour to feed a starter dough. Organic flour is expensive and needs to be sourced carefully and rotated correctly. Commercially milled flour can feed a starter adequately enough to produce consistent and daily sour dough loaves.

Fact – Sourdough requires time!
Sourdough requires what is known as the fifth ingredient (time) after flour, water, salt and leavening agent. Time allows sourdoughs natural wild yeasts to feed gently on the maltose in the flour and break down the enzymes and starches, thus producing a slightly acidic flavour and taste structure synonymous with all sourdough breads.

Fact – Autolyse or the delayed salt methods of production aren't crucial in the method of producing sour doughs.
Sourdough can be made adequately and commercially by blending all the ingredients together and allowing for correct fermentation time and temperature control.

Myth – Sourdough is best for coeliacs and those with gluten intolerances!

Fact – Sourdoughs don't need to be 80 to 90% hydration to produce what is commonly known as sour dough bread.

Sour dough can be formulated and moulded and baked freestyle without being proved in baskets or baked in bread tins. Hydration of 60% can be adequate to produce a sour dough loaf.

Fact – Yeasted sour dough may be frowned upon by purists, but it remains sourdough.

Many bakers will add 0.5% yeast to a sour dough leavened formula to aid fermentation, speed up the process, and guarantee end results which can be sold to the public.

Myth – The older the starter (mature) – the better the end results.

If the starter dough is active, alive and shows good signs of fermentation, it will and can produce a sour dough loaf. Maturity in a starter helps to fight the elements which can work against naturally fermented enzymes, more easily than a younger fresher starter, which just needs more attention and care in the process.

Fact – Sourdough is easier on the stomach than commercially produced breads!

Sourdough is easier on the stomach to absorb and breakdown, as the natural enzymes / starch present in flour has been broken down by the long fermentation process which makes the bread easier to consume and creates less bloating in the stomach due to the non – presence of commercial yeasts which can be as high as 3 – 5% in no time doughs.

The lactic acids in sourdough neutralise phytates in flour, and slow the release of glucose into the bloodstream, lowering the breads glycaemic index and preventing insulin spikes. The lactic acid also makes gluten more digestible and reduces the chance of gluten intolerance.

Fact – Sourdough is expensive!

In comparison to other commercially produced breads, sour doughs are deemed more expensive as they are tagged with the "artisan "symbol which defines the product as being supposedly bespoke – and thus requiring time and more input.

One London baker made headlines by selling their real sourdoughs at 20 pounds sterling (approximately 30 Aus Dollars) that many were shocked by as a normal factory loaf is 2000% cheaper.

The irony is – is that sourdoughs can be less expensive to produce then commercial doughs. If you take into account all the hidden factors, of not requiring any commercial yeasts, or commercial additives and special equipment, tank water as opposed to tap water if available, and a high protein bread making flour – which is what most breads are or can be made with, then the calculations added up revert only to the time element, and hand moulding.

In respect – basic sourdough shouldn't be expensive. It's only when other flavourings, additives, seeds, and additional old-world cereals are included as well as vegetables, herbs and spices that it then requires monitoring as far as cost control.

Myth – Sourdough requires technical skills to produce!

Sourdough is normally highly hydrated – anything from 60-80 percent, which calls for a slightly differing approach to handling and moulding. Because of the higher hydration levels, machines are not used to mould sourdough – unless the water content veers towards less than more.

Cane baskets – Banatons are used to allow the higher hydrated doughs their final prove, before being unmoulded and baked. The only difficulty / requirement needed – is just adapting to the softness of the dough and providing a more gentle but rigorous affirmation towards its control.

The more the dough is handled, the easier it becomes, and confidence eventually rules over skill factor.

Fact – There is no ruling/ governing body or regulatory requirements on sourdough!

Sourdough seems to have fallen into a mystique confine, of where it is somehow defined by phantom regulations, stating it must be a pure, organic, unadulterated, traditional, artisanal produced product.

Although some organizations such as the Real Bread campaign (UK) believe that sourdough isn't a brand, fashion, fad or bandwagon to be jumped on, but the oldest way of leavening dough's – and thus are pursuing that the law provides a certain benchmark and working guideline to its manufacture.

Now in time – no regulatory guidelines exist, and the real bread campaign body have been lobbying the UK government for an "Honest

Crust Act "and their argument is that industrial loaf fabricators, undermine the integrity of the word sourdough.

An Honest crust regulation act would mean that Sourdough remains free from any additives and leavened only by a live sour dough starter culture.

Australian bread can presently be labeled sourdough even if it's not 100% sourdough. The Artisan Baker Association are supporting a long overdue push to review the standard of breads labeled sourdough in Australia with the ACCC and FSA – and therefore help customers make better defined choices while shopping for correct labeling of ingredients, and without being duped into a false sense of uncertainty and misleading information.

Sourdough ultimately should be sourdough.

Fact – Fake sourdough is sold as sourdough!

"Sourfaux" – is the nickname been given out for breads which are labeled sourdough but are in truth non – sourdough. Vinegar and sourdough concentrates can substitute for the sour notes in sourdough but are ultimately damaging the brand mark of what sour dough stands for, what it is and should be. Purity and Honesty are not marketing traits and time isn't an ingredient either, but these three factors define sourdough and its imperative that, sugar, sweeteners, milk, yeast, oil, corn, dough conditioners, whole grains should be totally excluded.

Fact – Sourdough has a long shelf life!

Through natural fermentation processes, sourdough creates two main acids, one being lactic acid, the other acetic acid. Both these two acids in conjunction with each other help to provide a combative force against the buildup of mould and any other bacterial growth within the bread.

Acetic acid – or vinegar – is the acid which gives sourdough much of the tang,

Fact – Sourdough is an Art more than a science!

59. Sour Dough Answered

Making a sour dough requires a certain set of rules. These are formed to assist the natural fermentation process and enable the dough to become active and alive.

It is possible to rely on just adding the four ingredients together, flour, salt, water, and starter, but it's best to follow a system of additions which gives a workflow to achieving a desired finished dough.

Sourdough loaf (authentic)

Tank water (not grey water, which is disused water – and not tap water which contains chlorine and fluoride)

Organic flour (unbleached -no pesticides, insecticides, or chemical aging of the flour preferably stone ground)

Sea Salt – as opposed to table or cooking salt. Sea salt comes from evaporated seawater and is minimally processed so it may retain trace minerals. It also contains less sodium.

Natural starter – produced from a feed of flour and tank water – as opposed to commercially processed yeast.

Additions (feeds)

Wheatgerm, rye flour, potato

Method

Autolyse.

1, Strong bakers' flour and tank water mixed on slow speed for approximately 5 minutes.

   Allow to rest 20 minutes.

2. Add stiff levain and soft levain (mother) and mix on slow speed for 15 minutes.

3. Add salt and mix for 5 minutes slow, and 5 minutes on 2nd speed.

4. Bulk prove the dough for 2 Hours at room temperature. This can be done in a large plastic container lightly sprayed with canola oil, or on the covered table.

5. Scale the dough and hang up, resting for 15 minutes covered.

6. Shape the dough and place onto baking trays, moulds or cane reed baskets dusted with flour, rice flour or lined with a disposable hair net covering.

NB. Doughs can be scaled at 500, 600, and 850 grams. They can also be seeded or completely rolled in multigrain and seeds mixed.

The stiff levain is also referred to as a Chef or a pre-ferment. This is produced using soft levain, commonly called the starter or mother.

It must be produced in the afternoon/evening the day before and placed into a lightly oil sprayed bucket with a lid and allowed to sit for 1-2 hours at room temperature, before placing in the fridge before going home in the evening.

The following morning, this bucket is moved from the fridge on arrival at work, allowing it to come to room temperature a little before the dough making process begins.

NB. During chilly winter months, the stiff levain can be left at room temperature overnight, in place of being kept in the fridge.

Starter feed

One third Rye flour,

One third Whole meal flour,

One third Wheat flour.

Mix and blend the three flours together and keep in a plastic tub with a lid covering.

The importance of rye flour in the feed is that it will supply more nutrients and growth to the natural starter than just simply wheat processed white flour.

Organic flour is expensive, so many bakeries keep one bag of organic flour to feed their starters and use normal processed wheat flour to make the sour dough itself.

The whole meal flour acts as an indicator. Because of its bran content, it reminds you that you have fed the starter, as the specs of whole meal bran can be visibly seen with the naked eye.

The whole meal flour also contains more nutrient from the included germ.

Recipe

Stiff levain / Chef	1 K500g Strong Bakers flour
	500g Rye flour
	1 Kilo Tank water (tepid)
	50g Soft levain/natural starter/mother.
Dough	5K 625g Strong Bakers flour
	3k 625g Tank water
	113g Soft levain /natural starter/mother
Additions	142g Salt

Simplified Modern sourdough.

Using tap water, cooking salt, and processed wheat flour and a chef produced with starter.

Method

The previous day, prepare a chef with the starter, flour, and water.

> 1K800 Strong Bakers Flour
> 1K800 Tepid tap water
> 820g Natural starter

Mix on the machine with a dough hook or by hand. When well mixed, place into a lightly oil sprayed bucket with a lid and allow you to sit at room temperature for 1-3 hours before placing into the fridge on departure for the evening.

Remove from the fridge on arrival in the morning to allow the increase in temperature before the dough making.

> Dough   4Kilo Strong Bakers flour
> 100g Rye flour (optional-or replace with Baker's flour)
> 2K500 Tepid tap water
> 1 Kilo Chef

> Additions (added once the dough is developed)
> 300g Hot tap water
> 100g Table Salt

Allow bulk to prove for 2-3 hours, occasionally coil turning and allowing to develop before scaling, handing up, and final moulding.

Place in the fridge overnight covered with cloth or plastic sheeting and then place into the prover on arrival to work, to increase the temperature of the dough for baking, and allow it to fully prove.

Dust with Flour, score, and bake at 240C. with 5-7 seconds of steam.

Bake for approximately 25 minutes, using the flue/vent halfway to two thirds through the baking process to remove excess moisture and create a good crust.

Depending on the model of the oven and the capacity of the dough being baked, it will require extra baking time and monitoring.

60. Excess Yolks and Whites

It's a dilemma in pastry – excess yolks and whites,

    Simply increasing if not controlled, multiplying within our sights,

    So, it's worth noting, that excess yolks can be left adjacent to the scale,

    And incorporated into basically any preparation, -added simply without fail.

Yolks are basically fat, with a small amount of protein, and are an enriching agent,

    But they are also helping to bind, colour, and emulsify items within the kitchen pageant,

    Yolks can be added and included to any recipe, unless it's white such as meringue or icing,

    And they will not readily affect the format of products, if added with necessary sufficing.

Yolks can enhance, enrich, shorten, and improve overall quality of pastry goods,

    Improving texture, taste, and the eating quality of all manner of cookies cakes and puds,

    Appearance in colour, richness, (and gloss) – if used as a glaze – will all add to the aesthetics,

Using up those dormant yolks – without any guilty conscious of so-called culinary ethics.

Whites are a different story, and somehow seem to be in constant abundance,

As yolks are added to so many basic preparations, leaving whites as excess substance,

But all is not lost, as whites have a chapter of their own in the world of pastry production,

In fact, there are never enough of them, consumed somehow in practically every function.

Whites are used in most preparations, but it's the fluidity, which is its most important trait,

As whites are liquid, and subsequently give moisture, binding, and extension without weight,

They are as important to the pastry kitchen in preparation, as are herbs to a kitchen menu,

As excess whites can replace liquid in dough's, batters and fillings – while readily on queue.

Additional Yolks can be added to;	Additional whites can be included to.
Baked cheesecake mix	Cake batters
Doughnuts	Savarin paste
Brioche	Diluting fondant icing
Sponges	White bread roll dough
Choux pastry	Butter cream (Italian)
Shortbread, sweetpastry	Macaroons and Macarons
Short savoury pastry	Japonaise bases, Darquoise bases
Puff pastry	Sorbets
Butter cream	Icings, American, Royal,
Pastry cream	Egg whitewash for biscuits, pies, turnovers
Bavarois	Flourless sponges
Tiramisu	Cookie doughs
Egg wash	Mousses
Sabayons	Parfait ices
Cookie dough	Roulade sponge
Lemon tart filling	Marshmallow
Brulee filling	Almond bread
Ice cream	Base Souffles
Savoury custards	Pavlova
Portuguese Tarts	Crisp Dinner Bread rolls

It's worth noting, that if there is an excess of egg yolk, they can be placed into a bowl and covered with cold water and kept in the fridge overnight.

If not required, it is best to mix the egg yolks with caster sugar using 10 % of the weight of yolk. Mix thoroughly and then cover and freeze. This will then allow the yolks to defrost more easily and prevent any freezer burn which can cause small particles of the yolk to remain un-dissolved when using.

Excess whites not required can also be frozen. The only problem here is that the freezing dilutes the protein in the whites and they never fully whip up as strong as fresh or aged egg whites. The solution here is to scale off the required amount of egg white for use and add a small quantity of powdered egg white to if before whipping commences.

This will help to strengthen the whites, and they can then be used in the regular manner.

Allow at least 12 hours for yolks and whites to defrost. Working one day ahead and placing them into the fridge directly from the freezer, allows the defrosting to be gentler on the proteins and allows them to become ready for use in a more gradual and unrushed process.

61. Consistency

One of the main downfalls of many bakery/pastry shops is simply "inconsistency",

A key word in retaining customers' needs, satisfaction, trust, loyalty and cheerful glee,

It's possibly the biggest conundrum you must deal with and overcome to survive,

And it must be the hallmark on how business is perceived, judged, and kept alive.

You can't just swap, change, alter, re-arrange, or decide to not comply as need,

You can't just choose a finish one day, and then apply another as tomorrow's deed,

You can't just mix and match, to suit your own personal requirements and feelings,

And you can't just upturn; overturn, up skittle and format with unnecessary meanings.

Compliance here is the order of the day, if that's the message you want to convey,

Where uniformity, a little regimenting and clinical attention is required within the play,

Cleanliness, systematics, consistent finished products are the formats to help win the day,

As customers don't like inconsistency – especially while viewing daily products on display.

If you're selling coffee on your premises, then attention to detail is paramount and crucial,

As the regulars and gathering flock will ascertain immediately, with their seal of approval,

A coffee like cake can't be good one day, inferior the next, -whether taste, texture, look,

So, consistency within consistency is the order of the day, stamped in your reference book.

62. Sponge

Yeast sponges can sometimes be confused with sweet sponges in the bakery, and although the same title, they are two separate products.

Yeast sponges are basically pre-ferments. They assist the baker in many ways, by allowing the length of fermentation to take place either overnight or during working hours but without disrupting the workflow. They also assist in producing bread with more flavour, more activity, better crumb texture and better bloom. They also allow for less yeast to be used in the dough, allowing more fermentation from the yeasts and enzymes naturally present within the flour. This again gives a finished bread which is easier digested, causing less gas and bloating.

Allowing the sponge to stand like this also provides a natural gluten network development, which is like the autolyse method of bread making.

All in all, this is a much-preferred method of dough preparation by many mainstream bakers. It facilitates their workload by allowing the dough self-development, and it's just a simple case of finishing the sponge into dough once required.

There are various methods of making a sponge, but all require the same elements and practically the same ingredients. It must be remembered, not to overwork or overdevelop a sponge when preparing. Just bring the ingredients together and then cover and allow standing for whichever duration of time is required.

The process of this type of dough is termed "sponge and dough". Basically, this means that the sponge is made in advance and when required, made into dough to complete the process, with the additional flour, water and whatever other ingredients are required.

White pan bread (Sponge and dough)

Sponge

Ingredients	Percentage (of total flour)	
Flour	25.0	Mix to a clear dough at 21 C.
Yeast	0.7	Leave to ferment for 12-16 hours,
Salt	0.5	before adding to dough stage.
Water	14.0	

Dough

Ingredient	Percentage (of total flour)	
Flour	75.0	Mix to a clear smooth dough at 27 C.
Yeast	2.0	Allow for 30 minutes to relax before further processing.
Salt	1.5	(If no yeast, or less yeast is added here, allow for another
Fat	0.7	6–8-hour fermentation process, before working)
Soya flour	0.7	
Malt flour	0.2	
Water	44.0	

In this process it can be noted that 25 percent of the flour is made into dough and left to ferment for 12-16 hours. It is then mixed into a final dough with the rest of the ingredients, rested for 30 minutes in bulk, then divided and processed as required. Dough development in the sponge and dough method appears to come about by the well-developed sponge part reacting with the flour proteins in the rest of the flour during the final mix.

The above method is commonly described as a "quarter" sponge, indicating that quarter of the flour was made into a sponge and fermented overnight before adding to the other ingredients. The quarter method means that the amount of sponge added at the dough stage is about 50 percent of the flour weight in the dough. Therefore, rather than make a specific sponge for each dough, most bakers make the sponge in bulk and weigh of the amount of sponge required for each different bread.

Although the sponge and dough method is sometimes optimised today by bakers, in place of the straight dough with the addition of dough conditioners and improvers, which is quicker, easier, and less demanding – the sponge offers qualities of baking from a past era, where no chemical additions were required, and bread was allowed significant time to develop and provide a more natural, healthier, purist product. This is still extremely favourable with many artisan bakers today, who strive to achieve those exact results and depth of flavour within their breads.

Even though seldom used by many bakers, the process of using the sponge part as an ingredient in dough, acts like adding old dough from the previous day before.

The sponge is not added to aid dough development, but to add fermentation products to the dough and give a gassier texture to the final dough which is beneficial in crusty breads, where the crumb structure and crust characteristics are improved.

Doughs can be produced with "half" sponges or "three quarter" sponges depending on the time restrictions and types of goods to be prepared.

63. Sponge and Dough

1. The sponge and dough method are a two –step bread making process.

2. The first step a sponge is made and allowed to ferment for a period.

3. The second step, the sponge is added to the final dough's ingredients, creating the total formula.

4. In France this method of bread making is known as 'Levain – Levure". The method is reminiscent of the sourdough, however here; the sponge is made from all fresh ingredients.

5. The sponge method is used for three different reasons; taste, texture, chemistry.

6. Sponge doughs were used before bread improvers were invented. Texture is partly a by-product of the chemistry going on in fermentation, which activates the different enzymes, needed to leaven bread.

    (a) – (Modern grain – harvesting practices have reduced the naturally occurring enzymes that grains had in former times, a result of no longer used grain storage processes – so today small amounts of enzymes are routinely added to flour by the manufacturers, often in the form of malted barley, or sprouted grain).

(b) – (Proteases, dependent on their time of action, and concentration levels, soften the gluten in the dough, increasing dough extensibility, which allows the protein matrix to stretch out as the mix expands, thus leading to increases baked volumes and structure).

7. Sponges can be soft or stiff depending on the amount of hydration, and the amount of time they are given to develop, and their use. The sponge fermentation time depends on its temperature, and that of the surrounding area, the ingredients used, and the percentage amount of yeast. It ferments in a humid environment at 23-26 C where it may rise and expand to 4-5 times its original volume. When it falls it has reached 66-70 per cent of its allotted time.

8. A significant decision the baker must make, when designing such a formula or adapting a direct no – time dough (straight dough) formula or recipe, is to decide the sponge –to-dough flour ratio. While the relative amounts of ingredients used may vary, the method remains the same.

9. A three step, instead of a two-step, sponge-sponge-dough process results in a Spanish sponge type sourdough. The first salted sponge ferments to old dough, which is added to a second sponge, itself fermented for some time, before being added to the final dough.

10. In Italy, a sponge is known as a "Biga". This term is commonly used among Italian breads, such as the making of Focaccia, Ciabatta, Panini and Toscana.

Example of a 65% pre-fermented flour sponge and dough formula, using baker's percentages follows,

Sponge & Dough Formula

	%		%	
Flour	65	+	35	= 100.00%
Water	40	+	25	= 65.00%
Sugar	0	+	6	= 6.00%
Milk solids	0	+	3	= 3.00%
Fat	0	+	3	= 3.00%
Yeast	2.4	+	0	= 2.40%
Salt	0	+	2.3	= 2.30%

64. Gluten Allergies and Intolerances

Today we live in a society of instantaneous requirements and needs. Smartphone technology and fast-food living has made us dependable on instant access and speed. Gone are the days of waiting, unnecessary queuing, and abiding time to appreciate what we have. Wherever possible, we access a quicker route, a faster means, and a disregard for waiting. It has created a fast button, click button generation, where download times are more infuriating to wait for than red lights at a crossroads. Everything must be preferably no-time, quick, and now.

Hence the **"No Time Dough"** in bakery. From the introduction of the ADD process (activated dough development) and the creation of the Chorley wood bread process, quicker more adaptable methods were introduced into bread making, where high speed mixing, the use of bread improvers and emulsifiers, and no fermentation time were seen as the advancement in bread making processes and methods of production.

This saw the intervention of Hot bread shops, where doughs could be quickly processed, moulded, proved and baked, all in an open environment, allowing the customers to view, smell and purchase quick hot/warm bread straight from the ovens. The Don Miller Hot bread shops were a name synonymous with this process. This business concept lasted for several years, before the incurrence of bloating, indigestion, and the daily gluttony arising from consuming flavourless cotton wool textured bread. This bread did more damage to the baking industry than previous years, although many would argue it saved the baking industry by allowing home grown wheat's to be incorporated in dough making, instead of relying on imported strong wheats, plus it speeded up production and didn't require skilled and numerous bakers to maintain bread production.

The damage arose from people acquiring so called gluten intolerances, since bread was now under fermented, underdeveloped and matured, and not allowed to disperse the correct acids from fermentation to achieve correct PH balance. These intolerances led to a belief that many suffered from eating wheat flours and led to an increase that many were allergic to wheat and had become coeliac. The term allergy slowly replaced the word intolerance, and many became obsessed with the fact that glutton was the problem and that it had to be eliminated from the diet or at least reduced. The demand for gluten free breads arose, as did the influx of flourless cakes and cookies, all which were associated to the phobia of consuming wheat.

Gluten allergies and intolerances can be widespread, but the main culprit of these diagnoses is due to No time doughs. Add to this "the three percent yeast" addition to doughs, and the picture is more revealing. Three percent yeast is a pre-requiem in most no time dough's, to get the dough moving and becoming alive, but excess yeast when digested can also cause severe bloating, indigestion and acid within the stomach. Less yeast, and if preferable, no yeast or just 0.5% yeast would help to alleviate this problem, and many who suffer from so called wheat intolerances, might find that they are susceptible to yeast gasses within the stomach.

Although everyone has their own study case, it should be noted that this gluten intolerance/ allergy has only become widespread since the incorporation of quick bread making and increased commercial yeasts. The phobia of eating bread has now become mainstream as it's associated with digestive problems and weight gain. This in turn has had a knock-on effect on the baking industry and created a low disregard for mankind's staple food.

What is needed is a return to slow dough's, natural fermentation, and time. Time dough's produce their own gas naturally, and over a period provide their own fermentation. This also provides more flavor, better texture and creates better bloom and volume in baked goods. It allows for the starch to be broken down by enzymes present in the flour and in yeast when mixed with water, into simple sugars and break down or at least modify proteins such as gluten.

Flour and yeast contain many types of natural enzymes, but what is not required, as with bread improvers, is the addition of more enzymes, be it on the case of amylases, proteases, lipases and hemicelluloses, or the excess enzymes in yeast such as invertase, maltase and zymase.

An overnight sponge requires a lot less yeast than no time dough and was a preferred method of Bakers for many years, before the in surge of instant bread making processes. Even the domestic market was saturated with bread maker machines, where fresh hot bread could be mixed and baked within an overnight capsule, providing fresh hot bread to be consumed in the comfort of your own home. Again, bread was fermented minimally, and if eaten warm or still hot, could cause severe indigestion. This had reoccurring consequences on flour, and gluten, blaming it for its indigestive abilities and allergic reactions.

Although there may never be the perfect cure for gluten sufferers and coeliacs, one aspect that could benefit each one is a return to more organic flours, natural salts, correct fermentation, minimum commercial yeasts and the incorporation of breads fifth ingredient –known as time.

65. Inactive Yeast

As the name implies, Inactive yeast is completely inactive. It has no leavening power at all, unlike fresh, compressed, dried and instant powdered yeasts. The yeast is completely dead, but it has nutritional content and other properties which can benefit health. It's for this reason it is known as nutritional yeast, and many vegan and health recipes include this product within their recipes and meals.

Inactive yeast is made from yeast cream that has been pasteurised and sterilised, so that the yeast is dead, providing it with no power. It is sterilised around 121 C for about 20 seconds and then dried. It is a primary grown natural source of protein and vitamin B complex. It is a yellow to brown powder produced from baker's yeast grown by non – alcoholic fermentation on molasses and is inactivated by pasteurization during drying on steam heated roller dryers.

It contains glutathione which when mixed into a pastry formulation or bread dough, acts as a reducing agent on the gluten network breaking the sulfhydryl bonds and making the wheat flour and water mixture more extensible. Mixing times are reduced, thus reducing the oxidation levels improving and protecting the flavor of the finished product.

Inactive dry yeast, purchased in powder or flake form, replaces Sodium Metabisulphite 223 and L Cysteine 920, and is used extensively as commercial "dough or pastry conditioners", requiring no international code or "E" number when the raw material is listed on the label.

The usage rate is 0.1% to 2% of flour weight depending on the flour strength and application, with an approximate 12-month shelf life.

Benefits

1. Avoids distortion and shrinkage in baked products such as pizzas, bagels, pretzels, and pies.

2. Provides a protein barrier on the outside of baked doughs and pastries and helps support glazes and fillings, stopping the finished product from collapsing and going soggy.

66. Nutritional yeast

Nutritional yeast is another name for inactive yeast. It can be purchased from most pharmacies and health food stores with various brand names. Obtainable in powder or flake form, it is a good source of vitamin B12 and contains no whey which makes it suitable vegan and vegetarian product. It is used as both a food supplement and pet food ingredient, and snack foods such as pizzas, peanuts and many other foods where a typical yeast flavor is required.

Special vitamin yeast powder consists of pure, inactivated yeast, the nutritional value which is increased by a supplement of the vitamin's niacin, vitamin B1, vitamin B2 and vitamin B6. The product shows a composition of the yeast protein with all essential amino acids and is distinguished through its content of minerals and trace elements. The product has a pleasant, yeast typical taste.

Auxoferm special vitamin yeast powder has a good water binding and emulsifying capacity. It is excellent for compression.

67. Autolyse

The term "Autolyse" is probably one of the most important procedures in bread making.

Unfortunately, this method of making bread was brushed aside during the development of mechanical mixers, as prior to this; most bread was mixed in wooden troughs surrounded by one or more bakers.

The flour was hydrated in the water and left to stand for 20 – 30 minutes or even up to an hour or longer, thus creating its own gluten development without the rigorous mixing and gluten development.

With the advent of high-speed mixers, spiral mixers, and no time dough's, the autolyse method was dismissed as being irrelevant and not quick enough for modern methods of bread making. Hence it was regarded as something of a past era, and not in tune with today's requirements. Consequently, it has proved that this is not the case, as more bakers revert to this system of bread making, especially where slow doughs and artisanal baking preside.

The definition of the word "Autolyse comes from a French word "Autolysis" which is from the Greek words meaning "Self" and "Splitting".

Autolysis refers to the destruction of a cell by its own enzymes in flour (Amaylase and Protease) break down the starch and protein in flour. The starch gets converted to sugar and the protein gets reformed as gluten.

You acquire this normally when you knead dough to form gluten

– But –when you knead dough you also oxidise it (expose it to oxygen). Over oxidised dough (over kneaded) results in colour and flavour loss in finished bread which means it's pale and tasteless.

By giving the mixed flour and water time to go through autolysis on their own, you achieve the same results but without any of the unpleasant effect of oxidation. Additionally, an autolyse period gives the flour time to soak up all the moisture-resulting in more orderly gluten formation.

What this means for your bread, is that your dough will be easier to handle before its baked, and the result will taste better, have better texture, look better, and have better eating qualities.

The colour of the crumb is improved – the volume increased, and the overall appearance of the bread should be noticeably better.

68. A Piece of Old Dough

A useful thing, that piece of old dough,

    Sat in a plastic tub in the fridge, dormant, simply just laying low,

    Retarded, lifeless to some degree, awaiting its role call daily,

    Its reawakening timed, for the next batch of the dough making phases.

Who would have thought that something as irrelevant as a piece of old dough,

    Could reinvigorate, reactivate, and recycle, allowing fermented doughs to grow,

    How could it possibly affect the outcome to how products develop and mature?

    Be it in flavour, appearance, or crumb texture, not forgetting the bloom allure.

Such a simple practice, the baker's secret antidote to everyday perfection,

    Allowing all the hard work and homework to be instigated by this inoculation,

    That piece of old dough will perform what fermentation does over time,

    Introducing flavour, boldness, colour and beauty to whatever you're baked line.

It's basically a pre-ferment, a sponge, starter, conditioner, improver all in one,

A humble, simple, non-evasive and elusive addition, to whatever dough be done,

Quiet, modest, unobtrusive – to bring mystic and wonder to the science of baking,

When all it is, is daily necessity, utilisation and incorporation in the making.

So, the next time you make a batch of dough, try to remember this simple practice,

Don't utilise all the mass for baking, without a piece put aside for these learned tactics,

You will be amazed at the difference it makes to tomorrows developed yeasted dough,

And how it injects life and living into all the products it produces and puts on show.

69. Creams (1)

Almond Cream (1)

Almond meal (blanched)	1 Kilo	Creaming method. Either all together method and cream, or Butter and sugar together, add almond meal and flour, then eggs and lastly flavouring.
Butter (unsalted)	1 Kilo	
Whole eggs	1 Kilo	
Caster Sugar	1 Kilo	
Plain flour	100g	
Dark Rum	300ml	
Vanilla essence	50 ml	
P.O. Salt.		

Almond Cream (2)

Almond meal (blanched)	1 Kilo	Creaming method adopted here. Butter and sugar together, add eggs. Add dry ingredients and lastly flavour.
Almond meal (natural)	500g	
Butter (unsalted)	1 K 500g	
Caster sugar	1K500	
Eggs	20	
Plain flour	250g	
Corn flour	250g	
S.R Flour	250g	
Vanilla essence	20ml	
Rose water	20ml	
P.O. Salt		

Pastry Cream (1)

Ingredient	Amount	Method
Milk	1 Litre	Boil milk and half sugar infuse with vanilla Pour half onto yolks creamed with sugar and flours combined.
Caster sugar	250g & lemon.	
Egg yolks	8 half	
Plain flour	60g Cook out.	
Corn flour	60g	
Butter	50g	
Vanilla	one pod	
Lemon peel	2 pieces	

Pastry Cream (2)

Ingredient	Amount	Method
Milk	1 L 500	Half sugar with milk and flavourings to infuse. Boil, add cream. Reboil, remove spice and peel. Add sabayon of eggs, sugar and flours mixed, Cook out, add vanilla extract and rose water
Caster sugar	750g	
Star Anise	1 star	
Cinnamon pod	Half a stick	
Lemon peel	One piece to flavour.	
Eggs whole	9	
Plain flour	175g	
Corn flour	150g	
Fresh Cream	500mls	

70. Creams (2)

Butter cream (simple)

Fondant	1 Kilo	Beat the ingredients together in a machine bowl with the paddle attachment. When smooth and aerated, slowly add the water and vanilla and mix well.
Unsalted Butter	1 kilo	
Boiling water	200ml	
Vanilla flavour	20ml	

Butter cream (Custard)

Milk	500 ml	Make a custard with the milk, yolks and sugar, cooked out. Cool and add the butter while on the machine. Lastly incorporate the meringue and flavour.
Egg yolks	400g	
Caster sugar	500g	
Butter unsalted	2 Kilo	
Italian meringue	1Kilo	
Vanilla flavour,	30ml.	

Lighter French Butter cream

Egg whites	12	Make an Italian meringue with the egg whites and immediately after the cooked syrup, add the yolks. Add the butter when cooled and then flavour.
Caster sugar	1K400	
Water	400ml	
Egg yolks	20	
Unsalted Butter	2 Kilo	
Vanilla flavour	50ml	

Italian Butter cream

Egg whites	500ml	Make an Italian meringue with the egg whites and add the butter and flavour when cool
Caster sugar	1 Kilo cooked syrup.	
Water	300ml	
Unsalted Butter	1k 350g	
Vanilla flavour.	20ml.	

American Frosting

Pure Icing sugar	850g	Beat half the sugar, the butter, fondant milk and flavour together until smooth. Add the remaining sugar and salt beat until clear
Unsalted Butter	300g	
Fondant	140g	
Milk	60g	
Vanilla flavour	20g	
P.O. Salt		

American Frosting (chocolate 1)

Dark plain chocolate	250g	Combine the ingredients together and heat until dissolved. Allow to cool and then cream together well.
Muscovado sugar	60g	
Unsalted Butter	250g	
Condensed milk	100g	
Vanilla Extract	10ml	
Splash of Cognac or Coffee		

Chocolate Frosting (2)

Dark plain chocolate	500g	Melt the chocolate. Sieve the sugar and cocoa. Add the butter to the chocolate once cooled and incorporate the sugar and cocoa. Add the flavouring and cream well.
Icing sugar	160g	
Cocoa powder	75g	
Unsalted Butter	450g	
Vanilla flavour	30g	

Frangipane

Almond paste	500g	Place the almond paste and sugar into machine bowl and blend. Add soft butter, then whole eggs and essence and cream well.
Caster Sugar	500g	
Butter	250g	
Whole eggs	125g	
Almond essence	10g	

71. Pastry shop or Casino

Casinos are strange places. They lure you in to their enclosed world, where it's always daylight. There are no widows to gaze outside and ponder or reflect, there are no clocks on the walls in case you wondered what time of day it was, and there's never any sudden change in temperature to make you dress.

There's no background music, except for the clatter of money, throwing of dice or the circular rolling motion on the roulette wheel. The croupiers shuffling and quick dispersing of cards seems to be dealt with motionless and without any facial emotions.

There are hidden cameras, security staff at hand, and servers, bar staff and cash or winnings dispensers along with cloakroom attendants all under the gaze of secluded management.

Carpeted floors and nearly every amenity within easy walking distance, makes for ease of comfort, and provides a sense of relaxation, home from home feel.

Pastry Kitchens can be strange places too. They can lure you in to their enclosed world. Unfortunately, some are as small as a cubby hole, or what is also termed the spare room. Four walls with no windows and little airflow, unless there is a door entrance adjacent which can be opened.

Pastry kitchens can be an afterthought in kitchen design. They can be a segregated area within the building complex utilised as a pastry kitchen. They can be a space squeezed into an area never designed for its work role.

The one thing pastry needs is airflow. It needs a cool constant temperature, and regulated consistent lighting, preferably fluorescent or LCD lighting that is bright and reflected by white walls and ceiling. It needs a mounted clock on the wall, as time control is essential, timers on ovens and fryers.

The Pastry shop /laboratory need's temperature monitoring, and for this a wall thermometer / hygrometer is essential. Humidity levels differ with the weather, and this again needs to be controlled.

Time / Temperature /Humidity are the most important factors in baking.

Pastry shops shouldn't be reminiscent of a casino. Unfortunately, many are, in the sense they are coveted away in a world of their own. They need to be segregated from the main kitchen, but they also need to allow to breathe their own aromas, feel uncompromised by noise and heat, but more importantly, have a sense of freedom, creativity, time, temperature, and coolness. The aesthetics and format of the workplace must fall in line with the requirements of the job,

Composure, calmness, space, adequate lighting, air flow or air conditioning, fresh air, windows, if possible, temperature control, easy foot passage, essential fridge/freezer storage, correct appliances and ample work surfaces.

Casino or Pastry kitchen – when winning pays dividends.

72. Pastry and Perfume

Pastry has many marriages, whether its alcohol, bakery, or simply savoury cuisine on any menu. Pastry intermingles with practically anything and blends and adds taste, texture, and/or sweetness where required. It surpasses itself though with another addition, one which encapsulates what and how pastry is addressed and recognised, and what makes pastry instantaneously adored.

This simple evocative inclusion is "fragrance".

What makes pastry a perfume, is simply fragrance. This scent/aroma/fuel is a form of aromatherapy which allows pastry to outshine most other forms of cuisine, by creating in the atmosphere what most perfumers would refer to affectionately as a nose (French – le nez) or a fine fragrance evaluator. The job of a perfumer is very similar to that of the flavourists who compose smells and flavourants for many commercial food products.

Fragrance can be composed by single origin ingredients, or by blending others together. It can be produced by steeping, crushing, melting, baking, grating, pulverizing, juicing, roasting, steaming and boiling. Whichever mode of extraction is used, the odour which qualifies its being will always be noticeable. Infused vanilla pods, crushed hazelnut and caramel praline, boiled lavender or chestnut honey, grated fresh lemon zest, baked gingerbread, butter baked puff pastry, chocolate cake fresh from the oven, and steeped baklava syrup with orange, clove and cinnamon as reminiscent of Middle

Eastern fragrance where perfume makers are called "Attar". The list is practically endless, because items such as simply toasted coconut, boiled quince jelly, fresh summer strawberry salads, elderflower sherbet, and ginger infused sticky date puddings, are lingering and enticing fragrants to name a few.

Saffron which divides itself between savoury and sweet, as well as cinnamon, lemon balm, myrtle and grass, also work as perfume and can infiltrate the kitchen and dining areas with their pungent and yet gentle aromas. Fresh herbs too can play their roll, especially fresh mint, spearmint, basil, rosemary, and thyme, as well as all the spices and condiments used within pastry and the kitchen.

All in all, they make for an apothecary of the senses and create a perfumery and fragrant setting. Their strength and embodiment allow food to feed and nourish the senses, of which the most important is through the sense of smell. Its perfume is, and always will be the enticement and allure, and it will intoxicate the mind to being in a place of need, love and fulfillment. To that we are all grateful for the Earths source and nature, making pastry and fragrant perfume, a marriage of these elements.

The power of pastry scent can now be purchased in Eau –de –Parfum forms too which is an acknowledgement of this writing. Experimental and playful, the idea arose from an award-winning chef Fazley Yaakob, from le Cordon Bleu cookery school, together with the expertise of an 84-year leading perfumery house. Known as "Pastry" the company provides all perfumes of melted caramel, spiced chiffon, and crčme brulee, strawberry vanilla cupcake, and lemon meringue.

Many modern restaurants will gently spray their finished dessert plates with an intoxicating fragrant scent composed from the dessert itself, to help it receiving at the table, and allowing the guest to be instantly transported with the fragrance. This is very similar to smoking and smoked dishes served with a covered cloche, which is removed in front of the customer, allowing the fumes and aroma to be instinctively recognizable.

Fragrance will always be the key player in food preparation and service, and although texture these days is regarded as been more important than taste or flavour, and its five basic tastes sweet, sour, salty, bitter and umami, fragrance holds its own platform and pedestal as the most invigorating and enticing aspect of food preparation.

While humans have four genes for vision, there are over one thousand allocated to smell – which is also dealing with 400,000 recognizable odours in the World.

It may be worth noting quotes from the famous legend Coco Chanel,

"No elegance is possible without perfume;
it is the unseen, unforgettable, ultimate accessory"

73. No such thing as a last job!

Once you finished that, it'll be your last job,

But saying that, don't forget to complete the order,

And if you can, just add some finishing touches to that last cake,

So, it's ready for delivery tomorrow, or today if your quick!

And I forgot to tell you it needs boxing off,

So don't forget it's getting late, and the customer is fussy,

It might need some more fruits or glazing,

But leave that till the end,

And just decorate it accordingly with whatever fruits you can find,

Or if there's none left, just quickly pop to the supermarket,

And we'll reimburse you with the receipt on your return,

If it's not too late, and we have time to clean down,

Because tomorrow is busy and we will be pushed to get done in time,

So just do your best and try to complete,

And if you are struggling, you can come earlier tomorrow,

But on reflection try to make this your last job!!!!!!!!!!!

(Your last job – or your first job – or your ongoing job)

74. No-Nos – Not Yo -Yos

No prepping work on the scales

No moving scales around –keep stationery

No working directly over food bins,

No guessing weights for recipe formulas

No bastardizing of recipes

No faking quality

No wooden spoons in chocolate

No hot baking trays placed directly on working surfaces

No hot food placed in fridges

No raw egg in products which are consumed uncooked or unbaked

No uncovered hands in mixing unbaked goods.

No melting chocolate in microwave for more than
      30 second to 1-minute bouts.

No heating of fondant to more than 40C.

No liquid water-based colours in melted couverture chocolate

No sweetened cream with meringue

No over whipped whites in soufflés, mousses, and flourless cakes

No spun sugar on rainy days

No wooden rolling pins in the sink

No scraping/cleaning of small material with metal scrapers

No moisture surrounding chocolate work

No capping strawberries, preferably hulling them

No washing of fruits placed in fresh fruit tarts

No washing of fresh berries prior to their use, unless necessary

No washing of chocolate moulds and bread tins

No yolk or shell in eggwhites

No mixing of corn starch and cold starch

No placing of chocolate pens in the mouth when writing

No cutting on silpat mats with a sharp knife,

No cutting on a pastry sheeter/roller canvas with sharp knife,

No heavy handedness with soufflés and pastry work

No cross contamination on coloured chopping boards

No over sweetening, over decorating and over handling

No Placing hot pans/trays etc, on wooden benches

No over developing, over proofing, over timing yeast-based goods

No disposing of silicon paper after one bake

No items uncovered, unlabelled in the fridge/cold room

No incorrect rotation of stock

No glass, china, knives or electrical tools placed in a sink

No stacking of sponge sheets without dusting material in between

No strong-smelling odours, lighting, heating, moisture

    – when storing chocolate

No storing of goods/ commodities on the floor

No stored products uncovered, either dry or wet.

No chemical products stored near baking goods

No pouring used frying oils down the sink

No filled piping bags placed overnight in fridges

    –unless plastic and sealed.

No operating of any mechanical machinery without safety guard

No overloading, overworking, overlooking your machinery

No measuring jugs used as storage containers

No disrespecting of goods suppliers

No mixing old with new stock – (dry, fresh, frozen, chilled)

No cross – contamination, (raw with cooked, hot with cold, strong odours with mild odours)

No hot desserts served on cold plates

No frozen desserts served on plates that are not chilled.

No working rolled fondant/marzipan/pastillage on uncleaned surfaces

No open used containers placed back on shelves without being wiped clean

No omitting scraping down mixings to minimise surface areas

No scooping out glucose without a wetted hand.

No placing sugar thermometers directly into cold water from | hot cooked syrup

No opened used packet of baker's yeast placed into the fridge without re – compressing it.

No making laminated doughs without finger marking the turns

No placing of baking trays directly on the pastrysheeter canvas

No water on pastry brake/sheeter canvas when cleaning

No stacking of equipment and washed material face side up.

No standing with hands on hips, (wings) blocking passageway,

No walking around the bakery with hands in pockets

No running, no walking backwards, no knives carried pointed forward.

No balling up of scrap pastry work – especially laminated pastes.

No lemon pips allowed falling into cooked hard degree sugar,
>   (explode)

No knife blades placed down facing towards you

No masking of gateau /mousse bases from the freezer, without
>   removal of side acetate first

No washing of chocolate acetate sheets in a commercial pot wash –
>   best to hand wash and wipe dry.

No placing scrap chocolate into bowl/tank, reserved for writing
>   chocolate (Grains)

No churning hot mixes in the ice –cream churner-, chill
>   and then churn.

No placing items to bake into a cold oven –always pre-heat.

No retaining brushes in egg wash, in the fridge

No Donuts on floured trays before frying,

No placing pans to boil on the stove on a full flame, start gradually,
>   and then increase.

No boiling milk on stove without added sugar allowed sinking to
>   the base of the pan to prevent scalding – if possible.

No removing items from buckets with hands – use a plastic scraper.
>   (Exception for glucose syrup – wetted hand)

No placing of different shapes, sizes, weights on the same baking
>   sheet prior to baking.

No misplacing of oven mitts / gloves – keep stationery.

No dismissing the lore's of baking, because unlike cooking, baking requires statutory formats to achieve consistent end results, and therefore the rule book in baking can't be thrown out. It can be adjusted, tweeted, played around with, but it will always fall back to its intrinsic past.

75. Bakers Lung

White lung or "Baker's lung "as its industrially known, can be a common laughing yarn within Bakeries and Milling plants, especially when bakers coincidentally cough or joke about needing a cigarette break or some fresh air. It's a term which gets thrown around then forgotten about, until formalities are pre-empted, reminding staff of occupational hazards within the workplace and necessary safety practices.

But it can creep into the thought process and mind once any signs of breathing or respiratory problems arise. That's because Bakers Lung is a form of asthma, caused by flour dust, and it can lead to other symptoms such as dermatitis. The correct term for this condition is Occupational Asthma, and can include symptoms such as, wheezing, breathlessness, a tight chest, and coughing. More serious symptoms could indicate an asthma attack, which is basically wheezing and coughing becoming severe, becoming too breathless to eat or speak or sleep, breathing faster, a rapid heartbeat, drowsiness, confusion, exhaustion, blue lips and fainting.

If these symptoms appear to be worse during the working week, but ease of during days off and respite, then there is a good indication that asthma is related to the workplace.

Flour and enzymes that contain additives such as amylase are the second most common cause of Industrial asthma and rate extremely high in the case of severity amongst working bakers. Even though it's probably never discussed and bears little importance to those not involved in the industry, it is however a degenerative decease and can lead many bakers into early retirement, or possible illness.

Bakers' lung is caused by breathing in flour and grains, (wheat, rye, barley, soy, buckwheat,) additives and enzymes added to bread and baking, and other allergens present in bakeries such as egg or egg powders, milk powders, sesame, yeast, nuts and non-food allergens like dust mites, and other mould.

If precautionary systems are put in place, such as correct air flow, storage areas, mixing areas, ventilation, extraction, cleaning and health and safety practices, correct uniform, head covering and face dust masks where needed, and some form of health surveillance, then this condition can be controlled to a high degree, eliminating the need to take any drastic measures or controls. Simple effective procedures will create the safest and healthiest work environment to reduce or even eliminate totally the hazard.

Bakers' asthma and bakers' rhinitis are among the most frequent occupational respiratory disorders. These cases mostly occur amongst the predominance of small bakeries, where workplace conditions have hardly changed in recent decades. Work in such bakeries and confectioneries are often associated with exposure to high levels of air borne dust, especially during dough making and bread forming. The airborne dust mainly consists of flour, but also pollutants such as pollen, moulds, mites, and insect debris may play a role. Furthermore, there is considerable exposure to vapours, irritant or toxic gases in the workplace, especially to carbon monoxide, nitric oxide, nitrogen dioxide and nitrosamines.

Many pastry chefs and bakers can attract a lung condition known as "idiopathic pulmonary fibrosis" – which is a type of scarring of the lungs. The actual cause of the condition remains unknown, but over time the scarring becomes worse, and it becomes difficult to take deep breath and for the lungs to take in enough Oxygen. Unfortunately, it is a terminal condition which currently has no cure.

Bronchitis and Pneumonia are both associated with breathing difficulties and the lungs.

The cause of chronic bronchitis is usually long-term exposure to irritants that damage the lungs and airways. In the case of pneumonia, it can be life threatening, especially for infant's children and those over 65. Pneumonia is generally caused by a virus, bacteria or fungi. It's a serious infection which can damage lung tissue and affect the amount of oxygen that enters and carbon dioxide that leaves your body.

Unfortunately, Baking is near the top of the list of asthma – provoking jobs. It could be said that it's a hazard of the job and unfortunately, it's something you just deal with. That said there is no excuse for complacency in the workplace to avoid this invisible attack, which build its momentum on you over time. Management of whatever decree has a responsibility to provide work safe procedures –especially those which comply with regulated health and safety regulations. Because something is basically nonvisual, doesn't mean it's of non-importance.

Bakers' lung is a silent killer – be aware of it, be on top of it, and take all the necessary precautions to protect both yourself and your work colleagues. Many bakers, with guidance from their local doctors, have ended up as post men and gardeners on their way to retirement having suffered the conditions of the above.

It could be said that Flour is the provider, while flour dust is the unwanted grim reaper.

76. The Factor

In bakery, it's found that many bakers use yields, formulas and ratios to produce their goods, as opposed to just using a recipe.

Yield can be calculated each morning by using simple equations to achieve the correct quantity. With experience many bakers and pastry cooks can make simple instant calculations, such as doubling or trebling a recipe – or dividing a recipe in half or a quarter.

These simple equations though can come to grief at times and can also end with disastrous consequences. In bakery, it's paramount that wastage is kept to a minimum, and risk taking in calculating, is not a wise option, if mistakes are to be kept to a minimum.

Hence, we have what is known as **"The Factor"**.

By using the factor method, it is possible to amend a recipe to a specific yield with complete accuracy. All that is required is to calculate the yield, which can be easily determined by the unit weight required. Where one dough is used to produce a range of products, all that is required is to multiply the unit weights to reach a final required dough weight. Allow for small allowances such as loss or waste of dough during the mixing or processing.

To obtain The Factor, the following procedure is required,

1. Add all ingredient percentages in the original recipe to obtain a total percentage number.

2. Establish the required total dough yield.

3. Divide required dough yield by the total percentage figure. The result of this calculation will equal "**The Factor**".

4. Multiply each ingredient percentage in the original recipe by "**The Factor**". The resulting figure will be the new ingredient amount by weight.

77. BP is the Key

A little bit of baking in your croissant, a little bit of baking in your Danish,
    A little bit of baking in your doughnut, and a little bit of baking in your choux,
    It's a not a textbook rule, and many a chef may frown,
    But baking powder in your goods will make your products the talk of the town.

Some self-rising flour added to sweet paste, some self-rising flour for mud cakes,
    Some self-rising flour in your rough puff, and some self-rising flour in your scones,
    Baking powder in Pie Bottom paste and in roulades and emulsified sponge bakes,
    Baker's scones, muffins, cake doughnuts – and in all morning goods for coffee/tea breaks.

Sponge batter, cake batter, cookie dough, will all aspire to benefit from chemical aeration,
    As will crostolli, brownie, cupcakes, and most baked goods depending on their fabrication,
    It's an endearing product / by product, which should be within sight and easy arm's reach,
    It's a saviour and friend to assist and levitate– "It's off a higher standing" – as a matter of speech.

Of course, BP requires two elements, of which one controls the other to some degree,

An alkaline high PH and an acid low PH, working in conjunction to assist each other's plea,

Created by a British chemist, Alfred Bird in 1843, to assist his wife's allergic to yeast in Bread,

But the acid used, (cream of tartar), was difficult to obtain, and the invention was left short fed.

So along came Eben Horsford, a German educated chemist, suggesting a replacement be found,

And introduced calcium phosphate, (known as monocalcium phosphate) to create new ground.

And so, it is today, a format of two active ingredients, blended and combined with cornstarch,

Providing us with a unique product – and this gave the baking industry access to an opened arch.

NB

Now not to complicate the matter, there exist two types of baking powder available for use,

Single action and double action, which depends on your requirements and which you choose,

One contains two acids, the other just one, but not that they differ greatly otherwise,

Double action reacts as the products are mixed and again when heated for the products to rise.

Single action baking powder reacts once mixed, hydrated and baked, and is easier to control,

As more time can be given to production and finishing, especially when larger volume is in toll,

Double action better for quick breads, where the acids replace the yeast for the fermentation,

Here carbon dioxide is released faster through the acid -based reaction and chemical formation.

To complicate matters worse, the Americans call Bicarbonate of Soda "Baking soda"-confusing!

As most references refer to baking powder, as BP, not Baking soda – which can be deluding,

The two are totally different products, although the same family of ingredients, but segregated,

Important to keep the two apart and well labeled, to prevent becoming mixed or tainted.

Ingredients in BP today are,

- Sodium Bicarbonate
- Monocalcium phosphate,
- Sodium aluminium sulfate
- Sodium acid pyrophosphate (Commercial baking powders –not domestic)
- Cornstarch or potato starch

78. A Bakers Dream

Wanting to go to Thailand, but somehow ending up in Pie-land,

Wanting to see the pyramids in Cairo, but ending up using flour directly from the Silo,

Wanting to travel to the North and South poles, but ending up frying ring donuts, the ones with the holes,

South America, another destination on the wish list, but ended up making cookies piped with a twist of the wrist,

California dreaming, crossing the San Francisco bridge, but ending up monitoring temperatures of freezers and the fridge,

Europe was calling the lure of the vast continent, but cakes got in the way and somehow became more prominent,

To visit Scandinavia, and roam the fiords at length, instead it was early mornings and toil and drinking coffee at half strength,

Dreaming of soaking up the sun, cocktails, and stunning beaches in the Caribbean isles, but temperatures, stock taking, ordering, had to be noted and presented in files,

Then the penny dropped!!!!!!!!

I could bake and use the profession to travel, see the world, and prosper somehow, let it unravel,

There had to be an answer as to how to explore this vast and wonderful world of ours, not stuck or marooned working for hours and hours,

This would allow me to integrate, assimilate, appreciate, and communicate with fellow patriots of the trade – sharing the values of life, work, everyday occurrences, while still getting paid,

Then this had to be the best of both worlds, travel, work, companionship, friendship, trust and a unified bond, the Bakers dream became a reality, without the use of any spells or magic wand.

79. Unjustified

Another morbid muffin, another tasteless almond croissant,
Uninteresting Danish, flake- less butter croissant, lifeless slices too,
Insipid coffee and weak teas, vanilla slice without vanilla, rum baba without rum,
Welcome to 21st century patisserie, a sad reflection of how things have become.

Tinned apple or solid pack to knock up those tarts, scrolls and pies,
Where looks come before taste and the profession an unskilled disguise,
Knock it out quickly; knock it out fast, as long as we're finished by whatever quarter past,
No need to get sentimental, attached, committed- as business doesn't pay for finishing last.

And how has this circumstance arisen, and who is exactly to blame?
Is the customer's refusal to pay for quality, or is it just part of the daily economic game?
Proprietors will shout that there's a downturn in the economy, possible a looming recession,
Wage bills are too high, and commodities have risen to an almighty expensive concession.

Shortage of skilled labour, - nobody wanting to do the job, deskilling abound,
Where's it all leading, when cafes patisserie, resembles their competitors all around,
Where's the individualism, creativity, aspiring new ideas which makes life worth living,
It has to be addressed, removed from greed, compliance, and apathetic dismissing.

People become complacent, its common knowledge, and they become set in their ways,
They'll look for easy options, easy answers, and whatever's required to facilitate their days,
But they're not simply to blame for this downturn/ quick turn in the pastry/bakery profession,
Society in general has to ask them self too - as to why they've accepted this sad regression.

In the end it's the customers, who decide, as it is they who pay their money for our products,
But we as a profession have to also uphold the quality and integrity, not just line our pockets,
We have to maintain some form of commitment to producing fresh quality-based provisions,
Where taste, looks, and correct pricing, marry together, and leave us with ethical convictions.

It's a two-way direction where we have to meet in the middle, irrespective of our own judgement,
Because what's at stake, is the credibility of our profession, its continuation, its own enrichment,
Our trade doesn't have to be tainted, demeaned, diminished, belittled, patronised or unjustified,
It has to be honest and truthful, allowing customers to perceive our industry as being totally ratified.

80. Phyllo-osophy

Probably the best way to describe phyllo pastry and its characteristics amongst other pastes in the culinary world would be to assimilate it with the flatbreads of the bread World. It's so different in its appearance, its feel, its fragility, its ingredient content, its attentiveness and its applications, that it resembles no other paste produced in the bakery/pastry department. Its uniqueness demands a chapter of its own, and because its origins and roots lie in the Middle East, it requires in the western perspective, a different type of appreciation and understanding approach for its truly remarkable and versatile uses.

Strudel, Retes and Filo are basically off the same type of dough, while Warqa and Brick pastry which are slightly different in composition, are commonly associated with the same family of the thin, crisp, feathery, golden layers of pastry.

Phyllo more commonly known and spelt as Filo, is the purchased pastry that most cooks will turn to conveniently, when having to produce items either savoury or sweet, baked or fried. Convenient- because filo pastry made from scratch and prepared into thin translucent sheets, is a skill that requires both patience and skill. There is a time limit also to be added to the equation, as well as space requirement, because stretched filo will cover a large surface area which is best if it can be handled for best results within a 360-degree access.

Commercially produced Phyllo on the other hand is operated through automated pastry sheeters with a machine known as a stretcher using minimum cornstarch to avoid the paste congealing together during the operation. It's then dried under infra-red lamps as no cotton sheets or craft paper is used in machine made filo to absorb excess moisture. Once pinned to the correct thickness, it's rolled onto a spool, before being lifted and unrolled onto a table, where it is cut using a template to obtain the standard filo sized sheets measuring 33cms by 43cms.

Twenty sheets of filo are then rolled at a time, vacuum packed and then boxed and packaged for distribution and sales.

Here, filo can be frozen or fridged. Either way, it needs to retain its softness and suppleness and never be allowed to dry out until formed or shaped before baking or cooking.

Commercial filo can be purchased in various thicknesses and various sizes pending to some companies. Normally there is a thin filo and a thick filo. The thin filo being the most used for a variety of products, while the thicker filo is preferably used for making items such as "bugatso "which is a pastry of filo wrapped around a custard – (normally with the addition of semolina)- either in a parcel shaped pocket, or coiled like a snail shape, and then baked in a hot oven before being dusted with icing sugar and a touch of cinnamon dusting, and served warm – preferably as a morning good.

Another filo product which can be purchased is cooked filo. This is a slightly thicker version of filo and its advantages over normal filo paste is that it's quicker and easier to handle and can be quickly shaped in a dish such as Spanikopita (spinach and feta cheese parcel pastry) and Greek cheese pie –Tiropita. This is a Turkish filo paste as opposed to a Greek filo paste.

When working with filo pastry, a liquid fat is required to keep the sheets separated and crisp during baking. The fat most commonly used is liquid hot butter – the hotter the better – as it can be applied more thinly, preferably with a light brush stroke. The sheets don't need to be completely coated or saturated with fat, as long as there is some fat there to assist separation. The butter is best being a high quality one, with good butterfat solids content, minimum milk and unsalted if possible. If butter is melted and then allowed to set in a plastic container, it can be noted how the fat separates from the buttermilk by rising to the surface. If the fat on the surface is then punctured with a knife, and turned upside down, the buttermilk then can be caught in a bowl and used for cake making etc. what remains is simply the butterfat which if then melted is perfect for filo work. The more buttermilk there is in the melted butterfat, just causes the filo to be limp and non crispy when baked. It's for this reason that certain establishments purchase ghee for filo work as opposed to butter. Ghee comes completely pure without the milk solids and is simply just butterfat. This is then melted and used accordingly. Ghee can be slightly more expensive than butter, which is all that needs to be noted here, but again if used liberally; it can equate and balance out in price.

It's important to use the right fat for filo work to obtain not just crispness but also flavour . Mixing olive oil and in some cases vegetable oil with the butter will expand the butter usage, but it will also dilute and diminish the flavour plus the crispness of the baked goods. It's normally practiced as a cost cutting exercise, as butter is expensive kilo for kilo, but if hot butter is brushed on minimally, the end product will not create a product profit lost.

When working with filo pastry, a certain degree of care and attentiveness is applied. The filo mustn't be allowed to dry or become dry, so speed and care are essential. Only remove small amounts of filo required to accomplish one task before starting another. It's either that, or use a towel or plastic sheeting over the filo sheets while working with the remaining ones. Make sure any air- conditioning units are switched off, or at least on a very low fan usage, as they will make the filo pastry become dry very easily.

Filo is gentle, thin, semi -transparent. It can't be roughly handled, it requires care, and it needs thought. If handled correctly it allows you to perform many variations on a theme, and it will fold and bend and be compliant to your needs. Remember this pastry is ultra- versatile. It can be baked, fried, dried and crushed and incorporated in cake mixes. It can garnish, it can support, and it can decorate, and can be rolled, folded, twisted, pleated, bundled, and formed.

Filo is the one paste in the pastry department which is completely undermined and gets the least attention or recognition. It's normally brushed aside compared to puff, sweet and short pastes, choux and brioche, but yet it is one of the most important and intrinsically most difficult pastes to produce. It's easy to purchase filo in a box, but try making the same quantity by hand to the same degree of uniformity, thickness, size and shape. Then consider the task!

Interestingly, it may be worth noting that it can take up to 12 years of training in Turkey to become established as a Baklava Master and professional Phyllo Baker.

81. Bakery

Bakery isn't simply about bread. Baking in all its aspects, whether yeasted, un-yeasted, is simply a metaphor for products which are produced and made for human consumption on a daily basis.

As bakers, our profession is to provide –The crunch of our profession is to simply be provisionary for the want of others.

We provide for the needy, the hungry, and the masses. Our profession is the working, manual, physical domain, where seventy percent of the Worlds staple diet, is continually and daily manufactured.

Bakers are simply akin to the salt of the earth. They take from Mother Nature, kernels from cereal, which has been nurtured and farmed, then reaped and cultivated, before being ground and milled. They simply add water and salt and fermentation. In retrospect the job couldn't be any easier, but bakery demands fortitude, commitment, hardship, muscle, and drive.

It's no job for the faint hearted.

Bread unlike other foods can't be grown, it has to be made. It can't be simply unearthed from the ground or formatted together from products or purchases. Bread has to be born.

It has to be created – using stem cells taken from micro biological bacteria, which are fed and watered and structuralised using proteins in wheat to form a product which creates the most memorable enticing odour once freshly baked , and one which instantaneously connects with all of mankind.

Ask any individual, what bread represents to them, and then read their soul. Bread is part of our being, our wealth, our health, our connection with the earth, with clean running water, the environment, sustenance, and aid.

It's been our savior, our life –line, our means of feeding those in need, from the invalid to the poor, from infant to the aged, from enemies to friends, and most importantly with religious connection to the Bible and the divine spirit Jesus who stated to the World,

"I am the living bread that came down from heaven. Whoever eats this bread will live forever "

From the moment of his birth, this new God was associated with Bread, and the city where he was born –Bethlehem – actually translates to "the house of bread ".

With a history that stems over 6000 years, and a world with hundreds of varieties of breads, it's easy to dismiss what bread actually is, what it was, and what it will be in the future years to come. One thing is for sure, its core ingredient won't simply be flour, yeast or salt, it will and always has been, life itself. Bread has been the cornerstone for humanity throughout the ages, and its importance is a bearing for connection to our being, our planet and our survival.

82. Code Of Practice

Work cleanly, dress cleanly, and clean as you go.
1. Place items accordingly - "A place for everything, everything in its place".
2. Never throw items into a sink, place them underneath or aside.
3. Keep the sink clear at all times, until cleaning commences,
4. Don't run in a kitchen, it's foolhardy and extremely dangerous.
5. Wash your hands on commencement and completion of work.
6. Keep your language like your plates –clean, orderly and pristine.
7. Leave the kitchen as you would like to find it-preferably maintained.
8. Act professionally in order to aspire to greater things.
9. Value the profession for what you can add, not just take.
10. Panic and stress reduces work flow, not increases (more haste –less speed)
11. Try to work 2-3 days in advance of work flow and requirements –if possible.

12. Check fridges each morning to assess rotation and spoilage. (temperature logging)
13. Freezers need to be defrosted and cleaned at intervals in order to run correctly.
14. Keep all invoices and delivery data /correspondence in check and up to date.
15. Temperature and air flow-ventilation need to be controlled and monitored.
16. Maintain good relationships with suppliers, refuge collectors and sales reps.
17. First aid boxes, fire blankets and extinguishers are prerequisites for all chefs.
18. Stock rotation of dry goods and decantering prevents any harbouring of bacteria.
19. Leading by example will eventually win the day.

83. The Bakers Prayer

For what the day requires our bake,

Whether Focaccia doughs or Chiffon Cake,

Provide and grace us our practical deeds,

To provide goods, furnished with grains and seeds.

Allow the weather befriend us, night or day,

Time and temperature decreed by prayer and play,

Adequate water, nurtured starter, natural salt,

For finished goods, from whole meal, rye and malt,

Pure sweeteners of cane, beet, honey and fruits,

To overshadow chemical additions and other substitutes,

Maintain our vision, our goals, our drive,

With stamina, fortitude, perseverance our strive,

Loaves that bloom, cakes and cookies to consume,

Grant us sales that stretch from morning to afternoon.

Baking our vocation, sustaining lives throughout the nation .

84. The Cycle of Life

What are Bakers - without Millers
Millers - without Wheat
Wheat - without Grains
Grains - without Farmers.

What is Bread - without Flour
Flour - without water
Water - without Rain
Rain - without Dams.

What is Yeast - without plants
Plants - without roots
Roots - without stems
Stems - without foliage.

What is Salt - without earth
Earth - without a planet
Planet - without formation
Formation - without life cycle.

85. Bakers Tips

- **Doughs** The wetter the better – (Quicker activity and fermentation process)
- **Scales** Stationary, calibrated, charged – (Digital, Balance, but preferably not Spring)
- **Scaling** Always over rather than under – (No underweight loaves of Bread -weights and measures)
- **Equipment** A place for everything and everything in its place.
- **Flour** You work with flour, not in flour – (Flour is a dusting material)
- **Scoring** Bread lame, Razor blade, Serrated knife – (St George, St Andrew, Angled, Patterned)
- **Baking** Pre-Baking, Baking, Post Baking – (Spraying, washing, Seeding, Scoring, Proving, Glazing, Icing, Garnishing)
- **Timing** If you can smell it, it's basically ready- (Oven timers, Digital timers, Mobile timers)
- **Baking Trays** Scraped, brushed, oiled rag, sprayed- (Black Iron, Perforated, Aluminium)
- **Pie Trays** Cooled, brushed with a wire brush, tapped – (Stacked upside down, sprayed on use)
- **Oven Mitts** Live next to the oven – (Cleaned regularly or exchanged, gloves deemed unhygienic)

- **Oven** Deck, Rack, Convector, Tunnel, Microwave – (Thermostat, Flue, Steam injection, lighting, Brushed, Cleaned, Maintained)
- **Baking Paper** Silicon, parchment, greaseproof – (One Ream equals 500 sheets)
- **Starter** If it floats in the required water content -its ready to go – (live source, fed, nurtured, controlled – named as mother, culture, natural starter)
- **Mixers** Spiral, Artofex twin arm, Eberhard Single arm, Planetary – (In hot weather Artofex twin and single arm may require ice as well as water to mix the doughs, as they develop doughs much slower)
- **Provers** Humidified, Incubator, Dry, Prover retarder, Couche, Clingfilm/Gladwrap – (Clear plastic rack covers-waterproof, transparent, dustproof, seal covering -zipped/unzipped)
- **Small Equipment** Labelled, in close proximity to work table, – (Maintained, Organised, Protected)
- **Storage** – Segregated from work area, – (Cool, Clean, Well ventilated, Minimum lighting, Items above floor surface)
- **Flavouring** Essences, Extracts, Compounds, Oils, Condiments, Seasoning – (Golden rule- Precision weights in formulas) – (In Cooking, less is more – as seasoning can be added -but not taken away)

- **Proving Baskets** Cane, Silicon, Plastic, Wood pulp, Poly hand woven wicker, – (Fermentation proving cloth, Hair net, Collapsible silicone, Bannetons)
- **Commodities** Fats, Dairy, Dry, Fresh, Frozen – (Correct storage, temperature control, FIFO, Stocktake, Audit)
- **Cleaning** Daily, waste refuge, carboard removal, Weekly Deep Cleaning, Annual Contract Cleaning, Extractors, Vents, Ovens, Quarterly Grease trap cleaning, Pest control – (Sanitisers, Detergents, Disinfectants, Bleach)

86. In defence of sugar.

In their continuing rant against sugar and their belief of its betrayal to mankind,

A new voice is required, to take a stance and defend it by a petition that's signed,

What is needed here is the full picture, the true history, a global interconnected consensus,

Of what sugar actually is, and why this so called anti –sugarism, mustn't be broadcast on us.

If we're not careful, they'll soon be trying to stop cows from grazing on grass,

And items such as salt will be excluded from anything and everything in mass,

We have to defend sugar, its properties, uses, diversities, and connection to our lives,

This humble crop of cane and beet, part of our lifeline as much as bees and beehives.

"I quit sugar", "Why I won't give my child sugar", "I quit sugar for life", are titles in vogue,

See them in the high streets, portrayed in bookshops, victimising sugar as the rogue,

Its senseless captions, arbitrary comments, selfish quotes denying sugar its own voice,

When really all sugar has done, is to bring happiness to our lives with that added choice.

Of course there were masters of the sugar fields, slavery, empowerment and greed,

Making countries so rich, that it's an abonnement to discuss and make others take heed,

It's flaunted in depravity, a history that's tainted with corruption, battles and the deceased,

A time which should be remembered, for all the suffering endured in how it was policed.

But it's due to this, and all its toil, that sugar shouldn't be brushed aside,

Of all the lives that were lost, so we today can appreciate sugars sweeter side,

If we bypass this product on the basis it's tainted with death and suffering, as with meat,

We might as well cease to live, and condemn ourselves to a guilty conscious and defeat.

We should uphold the struggle and the pain endured by all those involved in its being,

We should be thankful and grateful for what we have received, not dismiss without seeing,

From this endurance came light to embrace us with sweet, fuel, alcohol, bio-chemicals,

Fortunately today without any stigmas attached to make us feel like everyday criminals.

There's no need to denounce sugar, no need to incriminate it to such depravity.

No need to stigmatise it as the devil, the black sheep, the plague of living society,

There's nothing smart, clever or intelligent, on portraying sugar as the grim reaper,

When basically on reflection, allow sugar -"in its defence"-, to be its own keeper.

Duncan 2016

87. Gateau Marjolaine

The word "Marjolaine" is actually a female name and most popular in France, but also Marjolein or Marjolijn is also related to Dutch, or the Netherlands. Its meaning or translation in French is "marjoram" which is a minty herb and flower.

How a cake inherited this name is down to one person and not just an "anyone" person.

Introducing- MonsieurFernand Point – the so-called father of modern French cuisine, the pioneer of nouvelle cuisine, and considered by many to be one of the greatest chefs ever.

Fernand Point is simply the next best thing to Escoffier. World famous in his time, he contributed many things to the culinary world, of which one is his book titled "Ma Gastronomie" which was a resource for many aspiring chefs, and is still used today. One of Fernand Points protégés was Paul Bocuse, who himself went on to become another one of Frances famous chefs.

Fernand Point,s restaurant La Pyramide , located in Vienne , near Lyon, halfway between Paris and the Riviera was Frances first three Michelin star restaurant, and over the years it became the central training centre for future three star chefs. It has been the host to royalty, celebrities, foodies and anyone with an interest in fine dining and gastronomy.

The original recipe for the Marjolaine cake was published in Ma Gastronomie, which was the first and only book Fernand Point wrote, and over the years it has taken on many variations and adaptations, as the written recipe is quite complex. It has been bestowed as the "mother of all French desserts".

This particular cake was often seen on dessert menus in many top restaurants and hotels in the UK, especially where dessert trolleys were common. Sadly, over the years it has seen its demise and is seldom ever mentioned or seen now.

However, it's worth noting, just how important this cake is.

Besides it taking numerous years for Fernand point to perfect, it is possibly the first layered and textured cake of its time. The Marjolaine set precedence for future cakes, where layering and building and texturizing became an important quest, in forming what we know today as the modern formatted layered cake. Even the opera cake in its simplicity, was a follow on from the Marjolaine.

Many cakes, especially desert cakes today are just a follow on from Marjolaine, – except they adopt discs of frozen jellies, cremeaux and cooked brulee, incorporated with thin layers of tempered chocolate or crisp feiulletine, alternating colours and flavours with the addition of mousse and fruit pieces and finished with mirror glazes etc.

Marjolaine is a simple format, but it has to be executed correctly. A little like the black forest gateau often seen here and there, the wording can be correct, but the makeup depends on which method and design has been assigned, in whichever establishment. All cakes can be re-arranged and changed, but sometimes, beauty lies in simplicity and a respect for its origins.

The Marjolaine cake requires four basic elements. Daquoise or Succes base, whipped cream, praline butter cream, and ganache.

Technically a cake, if made correctly it should be light and delicate enough to serve as a dessert. That was Fernands challenge, a cake that could serve as a dessert in a three mitchelin star restaurant.

Butter was always the intrinsic ingredient in Fernands restaurant, and not surprisingly it was used extensively in his cake, in the butter cream and also in the whipped cream as a holding agent. Butter cream can be lightened or transformed into butter cream mousse, simply by adding equal quantities of butter, butter cream and Italian meringue together gently. The whipped cream only requires a small amount of softened buttered added to it once whipped to hold it , especially if the fat content is lower than so called double or thickened cream.

The success or dacquoise is light and with little flour, but should contain toasted hazelnut and almond.

The ganache is a simple 1-1 ratio of cream and chocolate, with the addition of a little butter to hold it if necessary.

The rest is simply culinary engineering – Building, Layering, Leveling and Finishing. To execute the aesthetics requires minimum decoration. A little like today's layered cakes, simple finishes, clean lines, minimum decoration and complimentary colouring, textures and flavours.

Fernand Point set precedence for what is known as the modern layered cake, and his tribute and acknowledgement should not be overlooked, but recognised and appreciated in today's pastry world.

With respect and gratitude, Monsieur Fernand Point.

88. Life's like a Donut

Life's like a Donut, which circulates round and round,
Circumnavigating the days, but only clockwise bound,
Donuts are simple, as our time on this earth should be,
Uncomplicated, easy to digest, and that's the main key.

Donuts are in fashion, "a la mode", they never went out,
Donuts are everywhere, just following your daily about,
Donuts are a favourite, never mind what the age range is
Donuts loved by everyone, conveying happiness and bliss.

A donut resembles life as its simply a journey of fulfilling,
Nothing too complicated, difficult, stressful or unwilling,
Donuts convey a rainbow of colours, toppings, finishing's,
Resembling all humanity, parents, friends and our siblings.

Donuts are a gift, token, a validation of empathy, kindness,
Because that's what donuts should resemble, a virtue of us,
They represent everything good in this unforeseen world,
Forging love and harmony and added sweetness all swirled.

89. The Future

And what of the future of the Baking Industry – I hear you say!!!
What does it hold for the next generations, those still in play?
Is there a future, a trade which can both continue and flourish?
Or is it looming downhill, – whilst leaving masses to malnourish.

The industry's dead, finished -quotes that are often trumpeted,
Normally by minority, whose efforts have seemingly plummeted,
Those who have chosen to throw in the flag, and accept defeat,
Offering little but negativity, distortion, a vagueness with deceit.

If they took the time to consider what the industry has to offer,
Continuation of employment, craft, appeasing the daily shopper,
Food in its most basic form, its beauty, aroma and nourishment,
Supplementing the human chain, and not simply discouragement.

Baking is and always will be a means to an end- but with benefits,
As baking is an industry that doesn't over extend, or over commits,
It's simply there on a regular daily basis, supplying the necessities,
Never complicating or discriminating, wherever the towns or cities.

Will it become automated, semi-automated or an extension of AI,
Mechanical engineered robots, performing tasks that bakers apply,
Will 3D printers execute the decoration and finishing to perfection?
Or will it remain solely for operators to bake breads and confection.

People don't want to do the job anymore, early hours, poor wages,
Cries heard from "Jeremias of the world", whilst dismissing changes,
For them there is no shining star – no light at the end of the tunnel,
Doom and gloom providers, negativity as part of their daily struggle.

The job is simply what you make it, it will never offer a silver lining,
But it will enforce a sense of belonging, a structure while providing,
You only get in life from what you give, and with baking that's a fact,
A reason- meaning for baking, your own social communal contract.

Its difficult to grow tired off, somehow injected into the bloodstream,
You'll feel its calling, even during the hours, when knowingly unseen,
It a tough, manual, labour intensive commitment, once decided upon,
But it's an equally rewarding vocation, devoid of days feeling lost/won.

No job is easy, no day without its ups or downs, there is no free meal,
Pastry and Bakery addressed each day, there to test your zest and zeal,
Yes, an office job, a 9 to 5 with weekends off -is always another option,
But Bakery allows you to challenge yourself, the future and its tradition.

90. Thought Of the Day

Reliability is the only requirement needed on your resume.

If you can't clean- you can't cook.

Baking is about connection – not just perfection.

Bakers aren't Bankers and Bankers aren't Bakers.

You don't need social platforms to be a Baker / Pastry cook.

You need a sense of humour to survive the industry.

Le pain- or maybe the pain -you decide!!

The capacity of an oven dictates the work load.

Politicians have their own language, musicians too and Bakers theirs.

Rule one – make life easy for yourself – rule two- make life easy for others.

The essence of our work as Bakers and pastrycooks – is making others happy.

Bakery is more a vocation than a job.

It's a trade, a profession, but also a hobby, and a therapeutic pastime.

When working – everything should be within arm's length or short walking distance.

A place for everything – everything in its place.

The best recipe in life- is being good at your job.

Freshly baked butter croissant- probably the best perfume around.

If you enjoy your work- you'll never feel those aches and pains.

Pastry rewards you if you treat it with respect.

Cakes should talk to you; they should encapsulate you.

Bakery/ pastry isn't about impressing people- its about making them feel comfortable.

I like to Bake and being a Baker are two separate entities.

Bread time or Bed time – decisions, decisions!!!!

Bakery doesn't take prisoners- its a question of do or die.

Concise, methodical, regimental – the Bakers mind set.

Quantity, variety, quality provides notoriety – to win the day.

91. Xmas Baking

It's the season of baking –and its where ever you may be,
From the USA, Europe, Scandinavia, Asia, or to Abu- Dhabi,
It's a festival recognised though the four corners of earth,
Celebrating what's commonly known, as Christianity's birth.

Xmas baking can start well in advance, to avoid the overload,
And its best to focus on products with shelf life – use by code,
Xmas products if prepared and stored correctly, and matured,
Can actually last for more than a year, products well procured.

Panettone, Stollen, Yule logs, Christmas cakes, iced cookies,
They're all in abundance, preparing the season of good deeds,
Mince pies in their hundreds – thousands, gingerbread a flow,
The world of Xmas baking, where products shine, candles glow.

It's a demanding time, and can stretch you physically, mentally,
With Xmas cakes to ice, decorated, puddings steamed dutifully,
Every country has its specialities, its customary and a tradition,
Preparing Xmas breads, Buns, Confectionery, as festive mission.

The list of products is endless, with names difficult to pronounce,
Scandinavian Snebolde, Klobenboller -baked using kilos or ounce,
Ukrainian Perekladanats, Russinan Krendel, Polish keks swiateczny,
Bolo Rei in Portugal, Polvoron in Spain, their go to sweet or dulce.

What makes Xmas baking exciting, is its annual feat of provision,
Knowing that it's providing nourishment and enabling cohesion,
But it's basically a festive celebration, one which Bakers endure,
The season of harmony and goodwill, is there to act and reassure.

92. Natural Sourdough Starter

Sometimes referred to as a "Mother" or in French a "Levain', this ancient process of mixing flour and water together to produce carbon dioxide from the wild yeasts and spores within the air, is still used today in Artisan baking and throughout many of the mainstream manufacturers. It is commonly referred to by bakers as a liquid starter.

By mixing the two ingredients and allowing them to ferment, produces both Co2 and two acids, one being lactic acid, the other known as acetic acid. The lactic acid is basically the liquid which can sometimes migrate to the surface, and the acetic refers to the actual substance matter. Both play a major role in flavour, fermentation and preserving the bread.

Different flours can be used to make a natural starter, but commonly wheat flour is used. Some bakers prefer to use only organic wheat to ensure no chemicals or preservatives present in the commercial flour will inhibit the wild yeast growth, but this is not entirely necessary, as a starter can be produced with non-organic flour.

Spring –distilled water is preferred to for the starter, as opposed to tap water which contains chlorine and fluoride substances. These can be seen to prevent the growth of the natural wild yeasts present in the flour. This water is preferred to for the first two days, and then once growth is imminent, then tap water can replace the spring water. Note, the water mixed with the flour, must be at approximately 24 degrees C. (room Temp)

A starter has to handled carefully, gently, and fed correctly in order for it to work. It mustn't be allowed to be contaminated, knocked or banged around, and disregarded. It should be fed at the same time, with approximately the same weights each and every day for it to be completely active and work correctly. If not required, it can be placed into the fridge, where the wild yeasts will lie dormant, but after a while, if not fed, they will eventually die.

It's a simple process, but can easily be ruined or destroyed by lack of attention. Try to treat a starter as a pet, or a new born baby, and give it constant care and attention, feeding it at correct times and with correct amounts.

The process of a starter can be anywhere from 3 to 5 days, and in some cases up to 10 days for it to be ready for use. Additions such as organic yoghurt, boiled-cooled dried raisin water, or boiled cooled fresh onion water, or some rye flour can all assist in the initial development of the starter, and help to condition its growth. The bubbly, yeasty batter –like levain will give your bread a moist open texture, fermented nutty sour flavour, and an appealing red crust which is satisfying to the eye and taste.

93. Hot Bread

Hot bread, straight from the oven, is one of the most enticing aromas in the field of food preparation. Like the intensity of freshly worked couverture chocolate, or roasted ground coffee, it provokes an instant allure. For this reason, it is used as a lost leader in many supermarkets and shopping malls, where fresh bread is baked on a daily basis.

The attraction of the aroma makes for a desire to consume it instantly, and warm bread is a most pleasurable product, but, it is not wise to consume hot bread straight from the oven, especially in larger quantities.

There are benefits to cooling down bread before breaking into it, beyond the fact that "carry –over" baking caused by the heat within the loaf, means it still continues to bake after it is removed from the oven.

The gelatinised structure of the crumb continues to set as the loaf cools. The crumb will be gummy, if it's opened before completely cool. The crumb smears across the knife, and the alveoli are torn. It is also physiologically more difficult for the human tongue to taste flavours when they are still hot as opposed to at room temperature. This is why cheese is served at room temperature.

Bread is also considered more digest able when at room temperature, preventing bloating from excessive absorption, and the fact less bread is normally consumed when cool as opposed to hot. It is easy to consume larger quantities of a product still warm and easily eaten, but the problem comes in the stomach's ability to break the hot starch down.

The most interesting effect of proper cooling on flavour is "flavour osmosis". As a loaf of bread cools, the crumb contracts, creating a pressure differential that pulls outside air through the crust, infusing the crumb with flavour from the crust.

For example, as a well coloured loaf pulled from the oven cools, pressure decreases inside the crumb. The pressure differential is equalised by air outside being pulled in, and as the air is sucked into the crumb, it is filtered through a well caramelised crust.

Passing through the crust, the air is infused with the complexity of caramel and Maillard, depositing in the absorbent crumb.

If by contrast, warm bread must be eaten, then it is always wiser to tear instead of slicing it.

Before removing bread from the oven, consider three factors,

Colour, Weight, Sound.

Aim for a realistic baking time, but note that under baking will leave you with a damp, heavy, unpalatable, and possibly distraught structure, with limited flavour, and poor aesthetics. It will consequently have poor keeping qualities and be open to being easily contaminated by mould growth/rope.

Use a temperature probe if possible – and pierce the loaves looking for a temperature of 97.C for the loaf to be completely baked in the interior.

94. Gingerbread

Gingerbread is actually two words, not one, known as a compound word,
Originating from Latin- "Zingiber, via old French Gingebras"-as conferred,
It's a major staple amongst Bakers, inherited in most corners of the Globe,
And in 17th Century, Gingerbread bakers were a Guild, of honey and clove.

Gingerbread is as prominent today as centuries ago, history to be savoured,
Because the combination of spices, honey, molasses, is an aroma favoured,
When baked it fills the atmosphere with a sense of warmth and enticement,
Fuelling the taste buds, endorphins, creating an aromatherapy contentment.

Its history has been baked over time, with wooden carved moulds to shape,
Today there are cutters, stencils, and even domestic kits, avoiding misshape,

But in general, the same methods apply, using dough that can be rolled out,
Creating figurines, houses, displays, decorations, to showcase any walkabout.

Gingerbread is claimed to have been brought to Europe in, or around 992 AD,
By Armenian Monk, Gregory of Nicopolis, which are claims we don't foresee,
But Gregory Makar, as he is known, left Nicopolis, (modern Western Greece),
And travelled to live in Bondaray France, near Pithivier, 1000km north of Nice.

He stayed there for seven years until his death in 999, passing on knowledge,
Of Gingerbread baking to French Christians, called Pain d,epices in his homage,
Eventually Gingerbread migrated to western Europe around the 11th Century,
And since 13th Century, was made in "Torun"- which became Poland eventually.

Here it gained fame, and was then brought to Sweden by German immigrants,

And by 15th Century in Germany, a Guild was created by the Bakers merchants,

A Guild solely for baking Gingerbread, which foresaw how important it became,

As it was claimed to be medicinal, ease digestion, a treat- well before its fame.

Popular now in Scandinavia, Europe, it has grown to form global acceptance,

Where not only taste and aroma precede, but where beauty is in attendance,

Because Gingerbread lends itself to artistry, creativity, bewilderment, history,

It's a cornerstone for Bakers, pastrycooks, feeding children's minds of mystery.

Its long shelf life and connection to the health, allowed Gingerbread to flourish,

Being baked in countries all over Europe, eventually for the Americas to nourish,

Its as popular today as it was centuries ago, especially towards the festive season,

The most enticing confection around, helped form our human bonding cohesion.

95. A world of Gingerbread

France – Pain d'epices

Brazil – Chiriqui – Pao de Mel

Germany – Lebkuchen

Austria – Lebkuchen

Netherlands- Peperkoek (Speculaas)

Russia -Pryaniki

Poland – Torun Gingerbread (piernik torunski)

Czech Republic – Pernik

Romania – Turta dulce

Bulgaria – Medenki

Norway – Pepperkaker

Sweden – PepparKakor

Ukraine- Prianyk

Denmark – Peberkager

Switzerland -Basil Leckerli – Biber

Iceland -Piparkokur

Finland – Piparkakut

Latvia – Piparkukas

Estonia – Piparkoogid

England- Gingerbread (Parkin)

Scotland – Parliament cake

USA- Gingerbread

Australia – Gingerbread

Italy – Mostaccioli – Susumelle

Spain-Pan de Jengibre

Turkey-Zencefilli kek

China – Mi-Kong

Mexico – Marranitos

Panama- Yiyinbre

Israel – Lekach (Rosh Hoshanah)

Initially Ginger, the spice for which gingerbread is named, was cultivated over 5000 years ago in South East Asia as a medicinal agent and spice in cookery. The first recorded recipe for gingerbread comes from Greece in about 2400 BC.

Pepper was originally used in the production of Gingerbread – and that can be denoted from the wording of Gingerbread in certain countries.

Potash, Ammonia Carbonate, Bicarbonate of Soda have been the prime sources of aeration in Gingerbread. Prior to Potash, hartshorn was used (crushed reindeer antler). Ammonia bicarbonate is also known for bringing out the flavour of the spices used – not just as an aerating agent.

Potash is still a preferred raising agent for Gingerbread as it also releases flavour.

Baking powder will allow products to rise, but will not encourage the products to colour as in the case of bicarbonate of soda, due to the fact its counter balanced – alkaline plus acid salt and neutral starch. Its for that reason some Gingerbread recipes combine both leavening agents.

Gingerbread can sometimes be referred to a Cake, a cookie or a paste to form decorative confections.

96. Hot x Buns

Its Easter, and that means one thing only, Hot cross buns,
Whether fruited, chocolate or any flavour that succumbs,
Apple and cinnamon, mocha, lemon myrtle, orange glazed,
But the flavour is immaterial, more important to be unfazed.

When production starts, it starts, and rolls on continuously,
And it commences with working to a regime, systematically,
The process is simple, the baking timed, the finishing applied,
It's reminiscent and similar to cherry season, an annual guide.

Most Citizens believe chocolate surpasses HXB at Easter time,
But chocolate is Easter Sunday – hearing the church bell chime,
Chocolate lasts a day, where HXB reign indefinitely – non-stop,
Pre-Easter- Easter- Post Easter, -realigned to the Bakers shop.

It's the one time of the year, that Bakers rule supreme, officially,
Besides flowers and bonnets and palms addressing holy trinity,
Cakes and HXB are a rudimentary acceptance with Easter time.
Irrelevant of supermarkets selling them as New Year's Day line.

It's estimated that millions of Hot cross buns are eaten globally,
A trend where manufacturing has grown and increased totally,
With an estimated fifty flavours of HXB produced Internationally,
It's reinforced that HXB are loved and revered compassionately.

Whether toasted, non-fruited, spelt, brioche, or savoury HXB,
Maple toffee, lamington, not with dismissing the actual forerun,
It's worth remembering that the humble HXB dates from 1361,
A holy cross stamped on a fruit spice cake, marking the Holy Son.

97. Bespoke Hot X Buns

1. An enriched dough, – Scaled, Spiced, Fruited, Egg washed, Crossed, Glazed.
2. Additions of Rye flour and wholemeal flour give better flavour and texture. (Milk, butter, egg , sugar, salt, spice, flavour additions are essential)
3. Cranberries can replace a percentage of sultanas or currants.
4. Diced candied orange peel or dried diced apricot can replace dried mixed fruit peel-or a percentage of it. Dried dark cherry pieces are another option to be considered.
5. Dried fruits can be macerated in flavoured tea, or thin syrup prior to inclusion of the dough.
6. A little fresh lemon or orange zest or both make a welcome addition to flavouring the Bun.
7. Vanilla essence, orange essence, lemon essence can all be included at moderate quantities.
8. A splash of rosewater or orange blossom water can also be considered.
9. Mixed spice, cinnamon are the common spices used but a touch of nutmeg, clove, ginger or a touch of Cardamon can also be incorporated. Some bakeries add a combination of Dutch Cinnamon and Dark Cinnamon (Cassia plant).
10. Honey in the syrup glaze gives additional flavour – a small percentage – as does orange Flavouring or Golden syrup.

11. Raw sugar or a percentage of brown sugar can replace the white sugar to provide additional Colour/flavour.
12. Spelt flour can replace wheat flour for a more flavoursome bun, but additional gluten powder needs to be added.
13. A sponge and dough or a ferment and dough will provide more volume to your buns. A straight dough will benefit from a small amount of natural starter with the added yeast – or the inclusion of Some pre-ferment (chef) or old dough.
14. The white crossing paste is basically a combination of flour, oil, water or milk. The flour can be a self- raising flour or white with a small percentage of baking powder. Alternatively, a boiled roux can be made with the flour, liquid and fat, then reduced down to a piping consistency with more liquid. Sweet rice flour, oil and milk will also suffice.
15. The addition of a little gelatine and flavouring in the boiled glaze, with a piece of orange and Lemon Peel, cinnamon stick, star anise, will provide a tastier finish.

98. The Alternative HXB

- Jam Donut Hot cross buns,
- Blueberry and white chocolate Hot cross buns,
- Sour dough Hot Cross Buns
- Vegan Hot cross buns
- Apple, honey, sultana Hot cross buns,
- Brioche hot cross buns,
- Nutella and chocolate hot cross buns,
- Cranberry Hot cross buns,
- Asian Tangzhong soft style dough hot cross buns,
- Gluten free hot cross buns.
- Sticky date Hot cross bun
- Sour cherry and pistachio Hot cross buns
- Fig and Walnut Hot cross buns
- Dulce de leche and pear Hot cross buns
- White chocolate butterscotch
- Cinnamon and maple Hot cross buns
- Savoury Hot cross buns (bacon, cheese, chorizo, vegemite, marmite, herbed, cheese and wild garlic,
- Cheese and chilli cheese and jalapeno)

99. Tradition

Because hot cross buns are a festive food as opposed to an everyday common breadstuff, they should be treated likewise. A rich golden dough, heavy with spice and sweet dried fruits and sugar, make them special and worthwhile making.

Preferably toasted – as the name denotes- they are a bakers delight and should be heralded by customers as such.

The Greeks in the 6th Century AD may have marked cakes with a cross. In the Christian tradition, the making of buns with a cross on them and consuming them after breaking the fast on Good Friday, along with the crying "Hot cross buns" was done in order to commemorate the crucifixion of Jesus.

Spiced buns were banned in England when the country broke ties with the Catholic church in the 16th Century. However, by 1592, Queen Elizabeth 1strelented and granted permission for commercial bakers to produce the buns for funerals, Christmas and Easter.

100. Cookie

The world of cookies derives itself from the Dutch word "Koekje",
And translates to meaning small, little cake, made of butter /ghee,
Its a universal word, and portrays many applications and adaptions,
But basically, it's a sweet confection born from baking interactions.

According to history, first records of cookie, were used as test cakes,
By placing drops of batter into the oven – resembling cookie shapes,
Here they could also determine the temperature from the ovens heat,
Before proceeding with baking cakes -round or spread out as sheet.

From this arose the birth of cookies, like small batched baked cakes,
A new addition in the world of baking, where trial and error dictates,
Biscuits are different, in the sense they're slowly baked and are drier,
Where cookies are more moist, crumblier, chewier, larger and higher.

Its sometimes-difficult differentiating between the two, much aligned,
But cookies tend to contain more fats, sugars and finishing's combined,
They're heavier and denser and can contain a filling soft on the inside,
All in all, they're the new go too – the Instagram photogenic new tide.

Cookies now come in all shapes and sizes, all modes of taste, texture,
There's Bar cookies and others sandwiched with frozen filling mixture,
Rolled cookies, dropped cookies, and cookies shaped, coated or iced,
And finally, cookie dessert cakes, cookie towers elaborately disguised.

Giant cookies have now evolved, and double /triple chocolate chip too,
Caramel, Nutella, Ginger- cardamom, Cinnamon, to mention but a few,
With every conceivable filling around to project this insatiable appetite,
The day of the Cookie has dawned, to be consumed either day or night.

101. Cookie Directory

Cookies- a form of magic which encircle our lives and astound,
Comprising of natural ingredients, or a flavoured compound,
But basically, the foundations remain similar, and connected,
Only texture, flavour, colour, garnish, -keeps them segregated.

A. Anzac, Afghan, Alfajores, Amaretti.
B. Biscotti, Biscoff, Black and White, Bourbon Brown sugar, Butter piped, Brandysnap,
C. Chequered, Coconut, Choc-chip (double-treble), Cats tongues, Caramel, Cinnamon.
D. Danish Butter, Date,
E. Espresso, Eggnog, Empire,
F. Fig Newton, Financier, Florentines, Fortune, Funfetti, Flapjack
G. Garibaldi, Ginger snap, Gingerbread, Guyuria,
H. Halloween, Hazelnut, Honey, Hamantaschen.
I. Iced VoVo's, Italian almond piped, shaped, rolled, Iced Smiley face, Monkey cookies.
J. Jodenkoek, Jello, Jam drops,
K. Keylime, Kourabiedes, Kichel, Koulourakia, Kipferl crescent,
L. Lemon drizzle, Lebkuchen, Linzer, Lavender shortbread,
M. Maple pecan, Malted milk, Molasses, Monte-Carlo, Melomakarona, Macaron, Macaroon, Marie, Macadamia,
N. Nutella, Nemesis, Nice, No Bake fridge cookie,
O. Oatmeal, Oreo, Orange Italian, Orange glazed,

P. Peanut Butter, Persian Rice, Pinwheel, Pistachio, Pumpkin, Pretzel,

Q. Quinoa, Qurabiya

R. Red Velvet, Raisin, Rugelach, Rosketti, Ricciarelli – (Italian almond), Rout, Ratafia,

S. Shortbread, Salted Caramel, Sesame, S'mores, Snickerdoodles, Sour cream, Speculaas, Sable,

T. Thumbprint, Tex – mex Chilli, Turtle, Tararua,Tea,

U. Ube, Ugly Biscuit (Brutt-ma Buoni – or Croccantini)

V. Vanilla Butter Horseshoes, Viennese whirls – fingers.

W. Walnut snowball, Whoopie pie, White chocolate macadamia,

X. Xmas Cookie shapes, The X cookie

Y. Yoghurt cookie, Yo-Yo,

Z. Zucchini, Zwieback, Zimtsterne star,

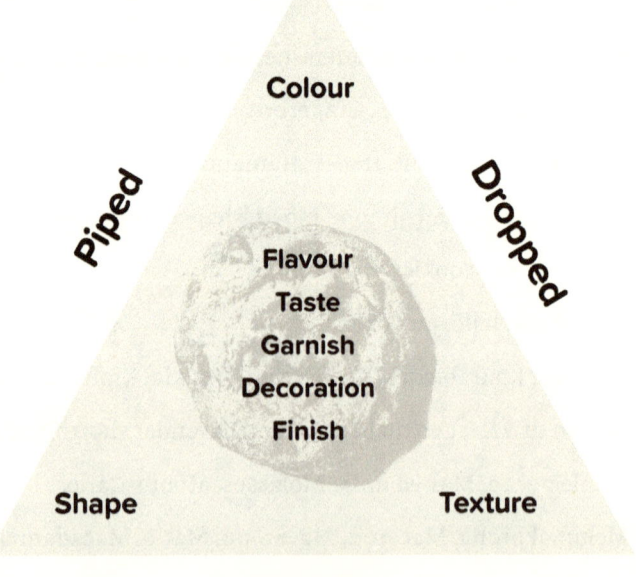

102. Befriend your Oven

It knows its task, it knows its place, it even knows its age,
It's probably taken for granted; it's simply there to engage,
Without its presence, just ask yourself – where would we be?
This friend of ours – applying our baking needs at any set degree.

Standing stationery ready to appease, it never shirks its duty,
Reliability, strength, and heat, all unified daily, nightly, weekly,
Dials, buttons and switches, for thermostat and timers, vents/flue,
Modular lighting, internal -external, and self – cleaning appliances too.

It's said that the life span of an oven is akin to a twenty five year mortgage,
Although ovens have been known to outlive their proprietor plus entourage,
Reel, convector, deck, tunnel, brick, wood fired, combi and pizza ovens too,
All with different names, dimensions, and some with glass doors to see through.

Rendering goods ready for human consumption, is what your oven will perform,
But it will also warm you on a cold winter's day, especially working dusk till dawn,
Airs you're washed metal material, preventing rust, plus keeping tea towels dry,
Covering a multitude of tasks and preventing dampness from being able to multiply.

It's your lifeline in a bakery; your support system, more than
 just your best friend,
As without it, there are no products to sell, no goods to provide,
 no means to an end,
So befriend your oven, your compatriot, your closest comrade,
 your friend in need,
And learn to accept you're nothing without its presence, its
 performance, its deed.

Never curse your oven, never foul mouth, or take its name in vain,
Treat it as your partner and friend, and in return it will help to
 self-maintain,
A regular clean, removing any excess residue, crumbs, spillage,
 or grease,
You'll see that it's more than an oven, something to worship,
 your own altarpiece.

103. Blind Baking

Blind baking – sometimes an awkward time-consuming necessity,
Par – baked pastry cases required, before the completion of the recipe,
Lining the bases to prevent distortion with some form of fixed weights,
Thus, allowing pastry to hold and structure itself, as the pastry coagulates.

It's a simple task, but can also be an arduous one for many a pastry cook,
Having to place items into the oven three times, to achieve a finished look,
But it is essential for many a baked product, especially those with
    liquid filling,
In order to prevent a structural collapse, and not have the
    contents spilling.

Even some dry fillings only require the minimum time baking in the oven,
So, pre-baking the tart case first, is a method that is safe, and also proven,
To achieve this concept and to adapt to completing the task correctly,
It's important to dock the pastry first, and line with a film covering carefully,

This can be gladwrap, parchment, foil paper, muslin cloth, or even
    butter papers,
And as the temperature never exceeds 160 C, there's no plastic
    melting capers,
The heat is absorbed by the addition of the weights and the pastry lining on
    the base,
This protects the gladwrap or paper from breaking, and simplifies this
    phase.

The choice of weight is open, depending on availability and what you
    have around,
And can range from dried pulses, cereals, beans or sawdust that's egg
    white bound,

Mixed sawdust, flour, and egg white made to a paste, moulded into
    rings and baked,
Once cooled and contracted, can be re-used over and over as a quick
    blind baking aid.

Haricot beans, lima beans, northern beans, chick peas and even
    split peas,
Are some of the items used, without incurring purchase of ceramic
    bean fees,
Even flour and sugar have also been seen included and uncooked rice
    grains,
But caution is required here, also as not to inflict on your profit
    margin gains.

If rice grains become entrapped in baked pastry, they become brittle
    and hard,
And could damage or break a tooth, if served unknowingly or simply
    of guard,
The best rule here is to avoid them and use items more visible to the
    naked eye,
Thus, reducing the risk and allowing you to have control, with food
    safety comply.

Lead pellets are deemed unsatisfactory today, and are considered to
 be dangerous,
Flour and sugar can burn or scorch in the oven, though done in haste
 being spontaneous,
Foil aluminium paper, can sometimes hold its own shape, especially
 if crushed together,
And foil cases need to be pressed down well inside a tart shell, to fulfil
 this endeavour.

Easier methods of blind baking tart shells, can be as simple as
 mounting in stacks,
This excludes the use of any fillings, especially useful for barquette
 boat shaped gaps,
Another suggestion used by many bakers, is to place the pastry on
 patty tins upturned,
Basically, reversing the process, then the fillings aren't required and
 therefore returned.

Another mode of blind baking is to remove the tart shell once
 baked blind,
Then place the tart shell over gladwrap which is placed into the
 circle lined,
This prevents the seepage of liquid if there is a crack or breakage in
 the pastry,
And therefore, no liquid can pour on to the sole of the oven
 within the bakery.

There are many entities to blind baking, and any aid can be used
   as a weight,
It's just a way to a means, to ensure the pastry is baked to
   the correct state,
Just as with everything in baking, it has its own entity and mode
   of production,
In the end, it's how you compensate for this, making it an easy one
   to function.

1. Baked egg custard tarts – deposit liquid filling into raw pasty bases in foil cases or tart shells. Freeze.
   Remove from the freezer once frozen, and place directly into an oven, preferably a convector fan assisted oven at 165 C, and bake until pastry is golden and custard coagulated. This method prevents liquid seeping or spilling in the oven once loading.

2. Take any liquid lemon tart filling and cook over the stove before pouring into a blind baked tart shell. This prevents a liquid seeping out as the lemon filling has already thickened. Continue to bake in a gentle oven until fully set.

104. The Face Book Baker

Connecting with friends, twittering the latest updates, simply saying hello,
Providing the news on who's who, what's what and info you should know,
Catching up on gossip, the latest culinary news and stretching your profile,
Welcome to techno baking – where your image projects that constant smile.

Baking blogs to digest with eating experiences of praise, or hidden fate,
News of pastry palettes, aficionados and whatever gadget they need to rate,
Recipes like confetti, a Wikipedia of baking news, access without purchase,
An Alice in Wonderland excursion, with a "hundreds & thousands "of searches.

Does your baking look better on face book, and does it speak the truth?
Are your comments justified, – and are they backed by evidence and proof?
Where will it take us on this social journey, or is it just some linguistic spin?
In the end it's your abilities and hard work, that determines how you'll win.

Face book connects and brings friends, colleagues and associates in contact,
With baking it's the same, connecting and helping to form a professional pact,
This is the era where we can assist and add our experiences to the forefront,
The face book baker can now be seen, heard and flow with the daily current.

Duncan 2011

105. Flat Bread

Leavened —or Unleavened, Bread as it all began,
Simple basic flatbreads, the staple food of man,
It counts for 2/3rds of breads consumption today,
Something we can't dismiss, as seldom on display.

Each country a variety, differing nation to nation,
But the basic rules exist, simplicity in preparation,
Because flat breads -a mainstream in households,
Are prepared daily, either flat or with simple folds.

The earliest flatbreads had origins dating 8500 BC,
Using coals which were fired by wood/ bark of tree,
It was simply ground cereals, wild wheat and barley,
Combined with water (Mesopotamia – or Iraq today).

All flatbreads have their national identity and names,
Some have fillings, are prepared with different grains,
Others have toppings, thicker or sweeter than others,
Either cooked in oil, clay pots, or through pitta ovens.

Flat Bread

There exists Roti, Naan, Chapati and Paratha in India,
Uttapam and Veechu in Sri – Lanka, – Kesra in Algeria,
Pita in middle east, Schiacciata and Focaccia in Italy,
Manakish in Lebanon, and in Afghanistan its Bulani.

Taftan in Iran, Hawawshi in Egypt, Injera in Ethiopia,
Farata and dholl puri in Mauritius, Philippines Piaya,
Xian bing in China, Turkish Pide, Cyprus Pitta bread,
Greek Pita, Socca in France, and Sweden its Polarbrod.

The list continues with too many to name and explain,
But just to say their names are unique -of which sustain,
Flat breads are not just wraps, sold as a simple encasing,
They're history and culture, to add as national embracing.

106. If Life Was A Cake

Cake Base	Birthdays	
	Weddings	
	Anniversaries	Take either of the three celebrations to form the foundational base.
Filling	Mind set	
	Emotions	
	Smiles	
	Feelings	
	Love	Create an emulsion of the five elements and blend together well.
Topping	Ideas	
	Thoughts	
	Choices	
	Decisions	
	Circumstances	Stir together and apply judiciously while retaining a level headed touch.
Garnish	Tears	
	Joy	
	Humbleness	Arrange in order of importance and inner feelings.
Decoration	Three G,s Gratitude,	Graciousness, Gratefulness and Apply with flair, spontaneity, freewill and conviction

107. Yeast Rules

Fresh Yeast

The oldest commercial form of yeast. Originally sold as cream yeast, fresh yeast today is commonly sold as blocks of cake or compressed yeast. It should resemble a cream/fawn coloured modelling clay, which should crumble in the hand when broken.

Best dispersed before use, it can however be mixed straight into a no time dough.

Fresh yeast has the highest moisture content of any form of baker's yeast, but also the shortest shelf life. It requires refrigeration and can last up to two – three weeks unopened. It is highly perishable and should always be compressed together once used to prevent quick decaying.

If fresh yeast begins to age, it can be utilised by using half fresh yeast and half instant yeast combined. (Important note: to decrease the weight of the instant yeast by one third).

Many bakers decree that fresh yeast has more flavour then dry/instant yeasts, but good flavour in yeast goods is derived from correct ratios, good fermentation, timing and correct baking.

Active Dried Yeast

Dried yeast was developed during the second World War by Fleischmann Laboratories in America, so as to assist sustaining soldiers and infantry men in baking fresh bread in the field camps. The active dried yeast was not as perishable as fresh yeast and therefore did not require refrigeration and had a longer shelf – life.

Basically, the water content is removed from the yeast cells during the production process, which sends the yeast cells into a state of dormancy. When required, these cells can then be re – activated with water, warmth and a little food – such as sugar in order for fermentation to take place.

Active Dried yeast resembles small cones / granules of yeast, which can be stored at room temperature in ambient conditions, without the problem of deterioration.

Instant Yeast

Instant yeast looks like active dry yeast, but the granules are smaller and finer. Its advantage of active dry yeast is that it doesn't need to be rehydrated before use. Its quick, easy to use and simple to activate. Many bakeries opt for this product today, as it is easy to store at room temperature, it's convenient and quick.

The only drawback is that its not as longer lasting as active dry yeast.

Osmotolerant Yeast

Also known as Osmophilic yeast or high sugar tolerant yeast, osmotolerant yeast is a strain of yeast that can withstand higher concentrations of sugar. It's ideal for products such as enriched sweet doughs, Danish doughs, Donut doughs and other Viennoiserie doughs such as Croissant, Brioche and also products such as kugelhoph and Coffee cakes.

All of these products have a higher content of sugar, and would probably slow down fresh yeast by overfeeding it.

Osmotolerant yeast requires less water than instant yeast used in lean doughs, and helps to provide a better fermentation process with much more yeast activation. Osmotolerant yeast can perform well at sugar content above 5% and as high as 25%, Salt content between 2-2.5%, and low water activity systems. It also provides a higher resistance to preservatives, provides higher tolerance to higher baking temperatures, improves machinability, and reduces mixing times by 10-30% compared to compressed yeast.

Osmophilic yeasts are commonly used in frozen doughs.

It resembles instant yeast in look, colour and packaging and stipulates which colour packaging is ideal for which percentage of sugars used.

NB Yeast, which is a living micro – organism – cannot be diluted.

(A living micro-organism can only be dispersed with in a liquid)

108. Artisan (Magic Hands)

Artisan is a paraphrase which seems to be highly in vogue these days.

In business it's the new catchphrase around to promote items which are produced by hand or at least partially by hand, under a particular label. The wording artisan expressing that the product is handcrafted/handmade, and without the use of modern confines of automated machinery. The end result being one of craftsmanship, where the results are aimed at being more bespoke than their counterparts.

This term covers many criteria, whether clothing and couture, jewelry, shoemaking, book binding, hairdressing, musical instrument making, the arts, building and construction, markets.

It's the 'In word" where exclusivity is expected, where time and effort are the hallmark, and where price isn't the deciding factor as to whether the product is regarded as the norm, or as an everyday requirement. To categorise it simply, the word Artisan is used extensively to market a business, a gathering, a collective, and its products.

But what exactly is Artisan?

The definition of the word states,

"A worker in a skilled trade, especially one that involves making things by hand, Craftsman, craftswoman, craftsperson, skilled worker- (Of food and drink) – made in a traditional or non-mechanised way using high-quality ingredients, e.g. Artisan cheese.

The word Artisan is applied a lot to bread making but less to pastry making, which is quite ironic in a way, as more apparatus and machinery is used in bread making than in patisserie work. Yes, pastry requires a lot of small equipment, and sometimes the occasional mixer, but a lot of its finishing is provided by hand, yet I have yet to see an "Artisan patisserie" as opposed to Artisan Bakery.

Bread produced with a natural starter, like sour dough, allowed to ferment and mature slowly over 16-24 hours, hand scaled, handed up manually, and the final shape moulded by hand, is labour intensive work. Whether it's placed into the oven on a slip, or peel or setters, adds to the intensity of the work load as well as retrieving it from the oven once baked.

It's a hands-on job, which can be simplified by machines. Looking back in time, the principles of the job haven't changed much, and the work can be modified, or it can be as it was – which means that the time factor will equate to a cost factor.

A supermarket loaf produced automatically and possibly not touched by hand will cost approximately one to two dollars, as opposed to a loaf of bread in an artisan bakery coasting three to four times.

This is where the argument arises as to the cost price validity.

If organic flours are used – they're more expensive than commercial flours. A lot of bakers will use the organic flour to feed the starter and use the commercial flour to make the dough, to keep costs down.

Neither distilled water nor tank water, won't really effect the costing, nor would tap water.

Organic salt or sea salt (non-iodised preferably) can be utilised in natural bread making but again there is a cost margin against everyday cooking or table salt.

Yeast is in a natural state, either a mother into a natural starter, which is added directly or made into a levain, with no baker's compressed fresh yeast in sight or instant dried yeast added, is actually a cost saving, as no yeast has to be purchased.

(Saying that, all bakers keep some yeast in stock as a backup for safety reasons, whether fresh or dried, and if some cases, throw a little into dough's made with natural starters to boost them)

The next factor is the mixing time which basically equates to commercial dough's – unless high speed mixers are used as in hot bread shops with no time dough's – and then it's all about fermentation time.

The idea of longer fermentation time is to provide flavour plus a natural breakdown of the starches/enzymes within the flour. This is where artisan bread makes its stand.

Its argument is, is that bread produced over time with natural starters, longer fermentation time, sole of the oven baking, produces a loaf of bread of distinct qualities ,character and appearance, and of course, greater eating qualities ,taste value and longer shelf life.

The argument of health benefits can't really be added to the cost value, as many may argue it's more agreeable for them to eat commercial sliced bread, plus that it's a convenience product, which allows for quick and easy access. Others argue that natural yeasts in bread making provide better absorption in the gut than those from commercial bakers yeasts used at maybe 3% or higher in the product.

Are people today more gluten intolerant or maybe just yeast intolerant is the question?

Artisan will always be a key player in attracting customers, and customers will also seek out artisan goods, as long as the concept is kept true to form. In today's era, people are more consciously aware of what is deemed good/bad, right or wrong , By that we are adhering and acknowledging sustainability, correct carbon foot printing, slow foods processes, use of local produce, accrediting plant based organics, animal friendly foodstuffs, the use of raw substitutes where possible, and last but not least, the incorporation of hands on, which for many equates to traditional, soulful, heart infused loved and cared for products, produced for you the customer by another human of the same stance.

Artisan reflects mother earth, but it's also teaching us that nature and its offerings need to be appreciated, cared for and respected.

109. Bakers Abbreviations

SF – Simple Factor

SD – Sour dough

MF – Major Factors

BA – Bakehouse allowance

MT – Mixing time

RH – Relative humidity

DY – Dough yield

TF – Time finished (mixing)

FT – Flour temperature

DRT – Dough room temperature

DTO – Dough to oven time

FDT – Finished dough temperature

ADY – Active dry yeast

HADY – High active dry yeast

RWT – Required water temperature

RDT – Required dough temperature

BFT – Bulk fermentation time

ADD – Activated dough development

NTD – No time dough

MDD – Mechanical dough development

WT – Water temperature

MRU – Measured required unit

RT – Room temperature

KB - Knock back

Fric – Friction

BDM – Bun divider moulder

F&D – Ferment and Dough process

S&D – Sponge and Dough process

SD - Salt delayed Dough process

ST - Stand time

$FDT \times 3 - (RT + FT + Fric) = WT$

$Friction = FDT \times 3 - (RT + FT + WT)$

110. Flour

For the Baker, flour isn't simply flour. Flour is to a Baker, what water is to a fish. It's the breathing matter, existence, life. Without flour there is no structure, no purpose of being, no products, and no sustainability. Flour is the lifeline, our quest, our answer.

There are plenty of flourless products on the market today, but the jest of most of our work requires flour, whether it is morning goods, bakes, afternoon pastries, petit fours, desserts and savoury items. Flour – "the poor man's gloves" – as it was named by confectioners, is also the dusting material that prevents adhesion, it's the glutinous mass when bound with liquid, it's the slurry that thickens, the food that yeast requires to develop, the basis of practically most prepared and baked goods, and also the decorating medium for an assortment of breads to enhance their appearance.

Although double in price per tonnage as compared to several years ago, bakers and pastry cooks still rely on this commodity as their foundation stone and lifeline. Whether purchased direct from the mill or via a supplier, one thing is sure, and that is this product does not improve with time. Flour does not age well; it doesn't like to be left to dry out and then resemble ash. Its moisture content is as vital to its performance as it is to the finished baked product, from the way it has reacted during process, how it has responded and to how it has baked. There are as many flours on the market as there are varieties of chocolate, each with its own protein count, moisture content, additions, and colour. The colour varies from a mild yellow creamy consistency to a practically pure white as in the case of a hi-ratio flour which has been milled much finer to absorb a higher quantity of liquid. Bleaching may have been the case in latter years for hi-ratio flours by the addition of bromate, but this is banned in many countries today and it's mostly the softer, lower protein biscuit flours that have the creamy fawn coloured shade.

The organic unbleached flours tend to be of the same shade, and depending on their origin and how they have been milled, (either stone ground, or roller milled) will dictate their colour.

Stone grounding retains some of the natural oils from the germ and the flavor, so much more than roller milled, and gives the flour texture and a slightly darker crumb colour.

Some wheat flours are blended to produce medium strength flour, but this can be done on sight or by the milling company, to produce a protein count in between 9% and 16%. On average a strong flour will contain anything up to 12 to 14% and even as high as 16% protein, where as the softer biscuit/cake flours can be as low as 8%. Again, all this has little effect on the product if the moisture content and life of the flour is low and too dry. A hand squeeze of wheat flour is a common practice by many bakers and pastry cooks as is a gluten test with warm water and a little flour to check how the flour feels and behaves. Stock rotation is vital unless your flour is delivered to a silo, where it will automatically disperse the old stock first. Otherwise store carefully of the ground, in a cool, dry well-ventilated room void of strong odours. Self-raising flour will not activate itself properly if having been left over an extended period of time, or left uncovered and open, thus allowing moisture in the atmosphere to attack the rising agents present. Gluten free flours must be kept in a totally separate area from other flours to avoid any intolerances or allergy requirements. Specialty flours such as spelt, quinoa need to be incorporated or used in the menus to prevent over storage and prolonged use by dates.

111. Sour Dough Answered

Making a sour dough requires a certain set of rules. These are formed to assist the natural fermentation process and enable the dough to become active and alive.

It is possible to rely on just adding the four ingredients together, flour, salt, water and starter, but its best to follow a system of additions which gives a work flow to achieving a desired finished dough.

Sourdough loaf (authentic)

Tank water (not grey water, which is disused water – and not tap water which contains chlorine and fluoride)

Organic flour (unbleached -no pesticides, insecticides or chemical aging of the flour preferably stone ground)

Sea Salt – as opposed to table or cooking salt. Sea salt comes from evaporated seawater and is minimally processed so it may retain trace minerals. It also contains less sodium.

Natural starter – produced from a feed of flour and tank water – as opposed to commercially processed yeast.

Additions (feeds)

Wheatgerm, rye flour, potato

Method

Autolyse.

1. Strong bakers' flour and tank water mixed together on slow speed for approximately 5 minutes.

    Allow to rest 20 minutes.

2. Add stiff levain and soft levain (mother) and mix on slow speed for 15 minutes.

3. Add salt and mix for 5 minutes slow, and 5 minutes on 2nd speed.

4. Bulk prove the dough for 2 Hours at room temperature. This can be done in a large plastic container lightlty sprayed with canola oil, or on the table covered.

5. Scale the dough and hand up, resting for 15 minutes covered.

6. Shape the dough and place onto baking trays, moulds or cane reed baskets dusted with flour, rice flour or lined with a disposable hair net covering.

NB. Doughs can be scaled at 500, 600, and 850 grams. They can also be seeded or completely rolled in multigrain and seeds mixed.

The stiff levain is also referred to as a Chef or basically a pre-ferment. This is produced using the soft levain, commonly called the starter or mother.

It has to be produced in the afternoon /evening the day before, and placed into a lightly oil sprayed bucket with a lid, and allowed to sit for 1-2 hours at room temperature, before placing in the fridge before going home in the evening.

The following morning, this bucket is moved from the fridge on arrival at work, allowing it to come to room temperature a little before the dough making process begins.

NB. During cold winter months, the stiff levain can be left at room temperature overnight, in place of being kept in the fridge.

Starter feed

One third Rye flour,

One third Whole meal flour,

One third Wheat flour.

Mix and blend the three flours together, and keep in a plastic tub with a lid covering.

The importance of the rye flour in the feed is that it will supply more nutrients and growth to the natural starter than just simply wheat processed white flour.

Organic flour is expensive, so many bakeries keep one bag of organic flour to feed their starters, and use normal processed wheat flour to make the sour dough itself.

The whole meal flour acts as an indicator. Because of its bran content, it reminds you that you have fed the starter, as the specs of whole meal bran can be visibly seen with the naked eye.

Whole meal flour, also contains more nutrient from the included germ.

Recipe

- Stiff levain / Chef 1 K500g Strong Bakers flour
- 500g Rye flour
- 1 Kilo Tank water (tepid)
- 50g Soft levain/natural starter/mother.
- Dough 5K625g Strong Bakers flour
- 3k625g Tank water
- 113g Soft levain /natural starter/mother
- Additions 142g Salt

Simplified Modern sourdough

Using tap water, cooking salt, and processed wheat flour and a chef produced with starter.

Method

1. The previous day, prepare a chef with the starter, flour and water.
2. 1K800 Strong Bakers Flour
3. 1K800 Tepid tap water
4. 820g Natural starter
5. Mix together on the machine with a dough hook or by hand. When well mixed, place into a lightly oil sprayed bucket with a lid and allow to sit at room temperature for 1-3 hours before placing into the fridge on departure for the evening.

6. Remove from the fridge on arrival in the morning to allow to increase in temperature before the dough making.

- Dough 4Kilo Strong Bakers flour
- 100g Rye flour (optional-or replace with Baker's flour)
- 2K500 Tepid tap water
- 1 Kilo Chef

Additions (added once the dough is developed)

- 300g Hot tap water
- 100g Table Salt

Allow to bulk prove for 2-3 hours, occasionally coil turning and allowing to develop, before scaling, handing up, and final moulding.

Place in the fridge overnight covered with cloth or plastic sheeting, and then place into the prover on arrival to work, to increase the temperature of the dough for baking, and allow it to fully prove.

Dust with Flour, score, and bake at 240C. with 5-7 seconds of steam.

Bake for approximately 25 minutes, using the flue/vent half way to two thirds through the baking process to remove excess moisture and create a good crust.

Depending on the model of oven and the capacity of dough being baked, will probably require extra baking time and monitoring.

112. To be Noted

Bread is the centre of humanity – its greatest invention.

Artisan breads should be made without accelerators or decelerators

Bakery doesn't take prisoners. Its either do or die

Baking is working to a systematic manner

Concise, methodical, regimental -a Baker's mind set

If you can't clean – you can't cook /bake

Bakers' mitts should be cleaned regularly

Recipes are like blue prints in your mind

The best recipe in life – is being good at your job

The capacity of an oven dictates the work load

If you enjoy work – you'll never feel those aches and pains

Cakes should talk to you – encapsulate you

Flavour, taste, texture – the essence of pastry

Pastry rewards you if you treat it with respect

I like to bake and being a baker are two separate things

Geometry – numerical order in Bakery

Reliability – the key word in Bakery

112. To be Noted

Baking is symbolic of love – when words are inadequate

Persistence – Don't sweat the small stuff

Baking is about connection – not just perfection.

Baking isn't simply about impressing people – it's about making them feel comfortable.

Freshly baked butter croissant-possibly the best perfume in the World

Le Pain or maybe the pain – you decide!

Bed time or Bread time – decisions, decisions, decisions.

Bags of flour were once 68-70 Kilo, then 25 Kilo and 12.5 Klo and now 5 Kilo.

Quantity versus variety , quality verses your notoriety

113. Fruitcake

Fruitcakes-they tend to orbit our daily lives
Similar to planets, but in a distant disguise,
Seldom seen, but only occasionally tasted,
Showing up, as when elaborately decorated.

It's possible to go a year without fruitcake,
Unless a wedding with a piece for keepsake,
And even then, its possibly a minute morsel,
A finger of fruitcake, to honour the proposal.

Fruitcakes unfortunately have stigma, Noted,
As they're associated with festivities, Quoted,
It's either Weddings, Xmas or an Anniversary,
Or wherever an occasion arises -Commercially.

The problems with fruitcakes are three-fold,
Heavy, rich, and an expense to be controlled,
They take time to produce and time to finish,
All of which incurs finance, costs to diminish.

Alcohol plays a role, and really can't be ignored,
Adding flavour, moisture, preserving as a record,
The fruit can macerate over time, increase in size,
Benefitting the baked cake, without compromise.

113. Fruitcake

The origins of Fruitcake stem from Roman times,
Even though it's associated as Anglo -Saxon lines,
Initially a mix of pine nuts and pomegranate seed,
With Barley mash added to sustain their feed.

Shaped into a ring, they were named as "Satura",
A dense sweet and sour mix, fit for any Centurion,
Taken on their campaigns as they were long -lasting,
MRE (meal – ready to eat) preventing soldiers fasting.

Europeans named it fruitcake in the Middle Ages,
But they became different, denser with changes,
They began ladening with honey, fruits and spices,
And any edible dried drupes and nut, as it suffices.

Eventually in the 1600s, sugar became prominent,
And it became an inexpensive addictive condiment,
It was conceived that soaking fruits in sugar solution,
Allows colour/ flavour of fruit, an added contribution.

It also accounts for fruitcakes to become preserved,
And the inclusion of alcohol/spirits, notedly observed,
All this added to the complexity and duration incurred,
But helped to create fruitcake, as knowingly conferred.

Regarded as the epitome of cakes wherever worldwide,
From the Caribbean to Sri-Lanka, traditions are applied,
The UK, Australia, New Zealand, India and South Africa,
The Bahamas, Canada, Italy, Portugal, Spain and Malta.\

Fruitcakes are steeped in history, time, taste, tradition,
From colonization, settlement and changing migration,
They've evolved into the everyday acceptance of being,
Just like planets, suspended, awaiting their sightseeing.

114. Scaling

Scaling is akin to tailoring, in the sense of made to measure,
Where accuracy, attention to detail, precision come together,
It requires concentration, calmness, application, eye contact,
As scaling is the invisible tailoring, unseen on garments impact.

Scaling requires fortitude, while adopting a calculative process,
As mistakes can lead to disastrous outcomes, or basically a mess,
Whether its reverse scaling, tare implication, or counterbalancing,
Its important scales are calibrated regularly, before commencing.

Scaling is the hidden application from which the product arises,
It's a needle and thread motion which then binds and comprises,
Clothes in general never detail the work involved in preparations,
The same applies to bakery, both incurring exacting foundations.

Spring, Balance, Digital scales can be used extensively in scaling,
Digital the chosen accuracy, where once weights were the thing,
Its important to monitor whichever method is derived to arrive,
As scaling is about consistency, the silent partner, a tailoring vibe.

Baking is a science, and scaling is the key to precision.

115. Fresh – The Bakers Deodorant

We use fresh eggs, fresh cream, and fresh milk too,
Unsalted and salted butter, when required on cue,
Fresh herbs for quiches, as tastebuds can distinguish,
Applying honest foods, in order for you to relinquish.

Bakery products need to be fresh, it's our hallmark,
The aroma, the scent, the texture -no question mark,
Its our duty, our commitment to honouring the trade,
Without fresh included, then customers are betrayed.

Don't deny, deceive customers the basics of our trade,
Which lies in simplicity, honesty, products self -made,
There's nothing worse than selling goods deemed stale,
Profiting from apathy or without any attention to detail.

Remember the code, the benchmark, the active input,
Delivering what only is Fresh, edible, the daily output,
Don't allow yourself to disperse old as something new,
As in the end, you'll be damaging the business you grew.

Fresh is your answer, the deodorant, customers adore,
Like a lost leader, of which people find hard to ignore,
Fresh will win the day, making your dedication known,
Accolades of Freshness, commitment reaped and sown.

116. Pastes (1)

Strudel

Baker's flour	500g	
Oil	60g	• Combine all ingredients together and
Egg	100g	
Salt	10g	• work well. Allow to rest brushed with oil,
Water (Luke warm)	250ml	• or covered with a bowl or plastic.
		• Stretch out on a lightly floured cloth.

Danish Dough

Baker's flour	1K 800g	
Yeast	60g.	• Make a straight dough. Develop well
Salt	25g	
Eggs	4	• Place in the fridge / Cold room to keep chilled.
Improver	30g	
Milk	1 Litre	• Laminate with cold – malleable butter.
Butter	100g	
Sugar	130g	• Three single turns.
Lemon essence	20g	
Vanilla	15g	
Butter (laminate, unsalted)	800 g	

Doughnuts

Baker's flour	2 Kilo
Water	750ml
Milk Powder	120 g
Salt	20 g
Sugar	160g
Eggs	5
Yeast(fresh)	150g
(Dried instant yeast-	75g)
Butter (unsalted)	350g
Improver	20g
Lemon essence	15g
Vanilla essence	10g

- Make a straight dough, Mix well.
- Place in the fridge / cold room to relax
- Scale doughnuts at 75g.

Quiche Dough

Butter (unsalted)	1 K 400
Plain Flour	1K 400
Water	1 L 600
Salt	60g
Baking Powder	60g
Plain Flour	2 K 300

- Cream equal Butter and Flour together.
- Then add remaining ingredients
- and blend well.

Choux Pastry

Water	6 Litres
Unsalted Butter	2K 600g
Salt	80gm
Sugar	120 gm
Baker's flour	3K 600gm
Whole Eggs	4K 800gm

117. Pastes (2)

Sweet paste / shortbread

Butter	3 K 500
Caster Sugar	1 K 750
Eggs	15
Plain flour	3 K 500
S.R flour	1K 750
Lemon essence	30ml
Orange essence	30ml
Vanilla essence	30ml
Salt	10

Sponge (Rest 30Minutes)

Plain flour	1K500g
Yeast instant (dried)	85g
Water	1L 400 (Tepid)
Divide dough into 4 equal pieces. Laminate each with 1 Kilo Butter.	

Croissant Dough

Bakers flour	5k 700
Salt	145g
Sugar	800g
Improver	90g
Milk Powder (skimmed)	270 g
Water	2L 500ml
Clear Honey	50g

Shortbread 2

Butter	3K750	Divide dough into 4 equal pieces. Laminate each with 1 Kilo Butter.
Caster Sugar	2K500	
Plain Flour	5Kilo	
Whole Eggs	5	
Lemon Essence		
Vanilla Essence		

The Wisdom of the Poet

Not all poetry contains wisdom,
but — at the heart of all wisdom — one will find poetry.